EFFECTIVE CO-PARENTING WITH A NARCISSISTIC EX

9 PRACTICAL STRATEGIES TO SET BOUNDARIES, SURVIVE MENTAL ABUSE & PROTECT YOUR CHILD'S WELL-BEING EVEN WHEN DEALING WITH MANIPULATION

STEPHANIE BARNES

© Copyright Stephanie Barnes 2024 - All rights reserved.

The content within this book may not be reproduced, duplicated or transmitted without direct written permission from the author or the publisher.

Under no circumstances will any blame or legal responsibility be held against the publisher, or author, for any damages, reparation, or monetary loss due to the information contained within this book. Either directly or indirectly. You are responsible for your own choices, actions, and results.

Legal Notice:

This book is copyright protected. This book is only for personal use. You cannot amend, distribute, sell, use, quote or paraphrase any part, of the content within this book, without the consent of the author or publisher.

Disclaimer Notice:

Please note the information contained within this document is for educational and entertainment purposes only. All effort has been expended to present accurate, up-to-date, and reliable, complete information. No warranties of any kind are declared or implied. Readers acknowledge that the author is not engaging in the rendering of legal, financial, medical or professional advice. The content within this book has been derived from various sources. Please consult a licensed professional before attempting any techniques outlined in this book.

By reading this document, the reader agrees that under no circumstances is the author responsible for any losses, direct or indirect, which are incurred as a result of the use of the information contained within this document, including, but not limited to, — errors, omissions, or inaccuracies.

CONTENTS

Introduction   5

1. Understanding Narcissism and Its Impact   9
2. Setting and Maintaining Boundaries   23
3. Effective Communication Strategies   37
4. Legal Advice and Custody Tips   49
5. Protecting Your Child's Well-Being   61
6. Self-Care and Emotional Support for Co-Parents   77
7. Personal Empowerment and Growth   89
8. Positive Parenting Techniques   103
9. Support Systems and Resources   115
10. Utilizing Technology and Tools   129

Conclusion   145
References   149

INTRODUCTION

One evening, my daughter sat across from me at the kitchen table, tears streaming down her face. She had just returned from a tense discussion with her ex about their child's school schedule. Her ex, a man who once charmed everyone, had turned the conversation into a battleground of manipulation and blame. My daughter felt trapped and emotionally drained, struggling to protect her child's well-being while navigating the relentless mental abuse from her narcissistic ex. Her pain and frustration were visible, and at that moment, I knew something had to change.

I am Stephanie Barnes, and I have witnessed firsthand the devastating impact of co-parenting with a narcissistic ex. My daughter's journey inspired me to delve deep into the complexities of narcissism, manipulation, and the challenges of shared parenting. With years of research and personal experience, I have dedicated myself to understanding these dynamics and finding practical solutions. This book is born from that commitment, aimed at helping parents like my daughter and perhaps like you, who face similar struggles every day.

The purpose of this book is clear: to provide you with nine practical strategies for setting boundaries, surviving mental abuse, and protecting your child's well-being, even when dealing with manipulation. These strategies are to empower you, providing clear actions to help you regain control and establish a healthier environment for both you and your child. I understand the pain points you face, the manipulation that leaves you questioning your reality, the emotional exhaustion from constant conflict and gaslighting, the inconsistent co-parenting practices that disrupt your child's stability, and the legal battles that seem never-ending. These challenges are real and daunting; you deserve the tools and support to navigate them.

What sets this book apart is its unique approach. It combines personalized strategies with an empathetic tone, acknowledging the emotional and psychological toll of co-parenting with a narcissistic ex. You will find real-life examples and case studies that bring the strategies to life, making them relatable and actionable. This book also incorporates modern tools, such as technology and legal resources, to enhance your ability to protect yourself and your child.

The book's structure is straightforward and logical. Each of the nine chapters focuses on a specific strategy, guiding you step-by-step through the process. We begin by explaining narcissism so you can recognize its tactics and patterns of manipulation. From there, we delve into setting firm boundaries, improving communication, and utilizing legal tools. We also cover essential aspects like protecting your child, practicing self-care, and fostering empowerment and growth. The final chapters emphasize positive parenting and building support systems to sustain your efforts.

As you read, I encourage you to engage actively with the book. Implement the strategies, take notes, and reflect on your experiences. Know that you are not alone in this journey. Practical help is available, and seeking additional support from professionals or support groups can make a significant difference.

Throughout this book, you will find real-life case studies and examples illustrating key points. These stories are meant to provide hope and show that positive change is possible. They testify to the resilience and strength of parents who have navigated similar challenges and emerged stronger.

The tone of this book is compassionate, supportive, and empowering. I aim to provide practical advice and emotional support, helping you feel seen, heard, and validated. This guide is both a resource and a companion on your journey to reclaim your power and safeguard your child's well-being.

So, dear reader, I invite you to take this journey with me. Let us explore these strategies together and find ways to create a healthier, more stable environment for you and your child. You have the strength within you to overcome these challenges, and this book aims to be a beacon of hope and guidance along the way.

UNDERSTANDING NARCISSISM AND ITS IMPACT

When my daughter's ex began to twist and turn every conversation into a labyrinthine argument, she often questioned her sanity. One day, after yet another heated exchange over something as simple as their child's bath time, she confided in me that she felt like she was caught in an emotional whirlwind. Her ex's constant need for control and admiration left her feeling small and insignificant. It became clear that we needed to understand the root cause of these behaviors to find a way out of this chaos. This chapter aims to help you do just that by diving into the core traits of narcissistic personality disorder (NPD) and how they manifest in co-parenting dynamics.

1.1 IDENTIFYING NARCISSISTIC TRAITS

Narcissistic Personality Disorder (NPD) is more than just having an inflated ego. According to the Mayo Clinic, it is a mental condition characterized by a pervasive pattern of grandiosity, a deep need for excessive attention and admiration, troubled relationships, and a lack of empathy for others. These traits often wreak havoc in co-parenting situations, making it crucial to identify and understand them early on.

Individuals with this trait often perceive themselves as superior, expecting to be acknowledged as such, even without commendable achievements. This trait significantly impacts co-parenting dynamics, leading to behaviors that diminish your parenting efforts. For instance, your ex may frequently criticize your decisions regarding your child's education or health care, positioning themselves as the more competent parent without any factual basis. This grandiosity can manifest in co-parenting as a constant need to undermine your parenting decisions, always asserting that they know better. For example, your ex might constantly belittle your choices, making you feel incompetent.

Lack of empathy is another defining characteristic of narcissists. They have difficulty recognizing or caring about the feelings and needs of others. In a co-parenting situation, this can mean ignoring the emotional well-being of the child. Your ex might focus solely on their own desires, disregarding how their actions affect your child. For instance, they might plan activities without considering your child's schedule or emotional state, leaving you to manage the fallout.

The need for excessive admiration is also prevalent among narcissists. They crave constant validation and will go to great lengths to receive it. This can translate into a co-parenting scenario where your ex continuously seeks praise for minimal parenting efforts while criticizing you to boost their image. They might boast about attending a single parent-teacher meeting while disregarding your day-to-day involvement.

A sense of entitlement often accompanies these traits. Narcissists believe they deserve special treatment and expect others to comply with their demands. In co-parenting, this can result in your ex feeling entitled to change visitation schedules at the last minute or make unilateral decisions about your child's upbringing. They operate under the assumption that their needs and desires should take precedence over yours and even your child's.

It's important to recognize that narcissism exists on a spectrum. Not all individuals with narcissistic traits will exhibit them to the same degree. Some may show occasional signs, while others might consistently display these behaviors in destructive ways. Understanding this spectrum can help you gauge the severity of your ex's narcissistic traits and tailor your coping strategies accordingly.

In co-parenting, these traits often manifest in specific, damaging ways. For instance, dismissing the other parent's opinions is common. Your ex may outright refuse to consider your input on important decisions, leaving you feeling marginalized. Another frequent behavior is ignoring the child's need to focus on their own. They might prioritize their convenience over what's best for the child, such as insisting on custody arrangements that disrupt the child's routine. Manipulating schedules for personal gain is also a tactic used by narcissists. They might frequently request changes to the visitation schedule to suit their plans, with little regard for the disruption it causes.

Recognizing these traits early can make a significant difference in how you navigate co-parenting. Observing patterns of behavior over time can help you identify when your ex is acting out of narcissistic tendencies rather than genuine concern for your child. Keeping a journal of these behaviors can be incredibly useful, not just for your clarity, but also for any legal proceedings. If necessary, seeking professional evaluations can provide a more formal understanding of your ex's behavior, offering you stronger grounds for taking specific actions.

Understanding and identifying narcissistic traits is the first step in reclaiming control and protecting you and your child's well-being. By recognizing these behaviors, you can begin to develop effective coping strategies, set firm boundaries, and navigate the complexities of co-parenting with a narcissist.

1.2 THE PSYCHOLOGICAL IMPACT OF NARCISSISTIC ABUSE

Narcissistic abuse is a particularly insidious form of emotional abuse characterized by constant criticism, emotional manipulation, and isolation from support systems. Unlike other forms of emotional abuse, narcissistic abuse is often subtle, making it harder to recognize and even more challenging to escape. A narcissist's constant criticism can erode your self-esteem over time. They might belittle your parenting choices, making you feel inadequate and unsure of your capabilities. This constant barrage of negativity leaves you questioning your worth and doubting your decisions, creating a cycle of self-doubt and insecurity.

Emotional manipulation is another hallmark of narcissistic abuse. Narcissists are skilled at twisting facts and distorting reality to suit their needs. They might use guilt trips to make you comply with their demands or gaslight you into believing that you are the problem. This manipulation can leave you feeling confused and emotionally drained. For instance, they might claim that you are overreacting or being unreasonable, even when your concerns are valid. This constant emotional tug-of-war takes a toll on your mental health, leaving you feeling trapped and powerless.

Isolation from support systems is a common tactic used by narcissists to maintain control. They might discourage you from seeking help from friends and family, making you feel isolated and alone. By cutting you off from your support network, they ensure that you remain dependent on them, further tightening their grip on your life. This isolation can be particularly damaging as it prevents you from gaining perspective and receiving the emotional support you desperately need.

The short-term psychological effects of narcissistic abuse can be overwhelming. Anxiety and depression are common, as the constant stress and emotional turmoil take a toll on your mental health. You might find yourself feeling anxious about interactions with your ex, always on edge and waiting for the next conflict. Depression can set in as you struggle to cope with the emotional abuse, leading to feelings of hopelessness and despair. Over time, these short-term effects can evolve into long-term psychological issues. Prolonged exposure to narcissistic abuse can lead to chronic low self-esteem and self-doubt. You might start to internalize the negative messages from your ex, believing that you are unworthy and incapable. This can affect all areas of your life, from your career to your relationships, as you struggle with a diminished sense of self-worth.

The impact on children can be equally devastating. For example, a mother who is constantly undermined in front of her children may notice that they start to question her authority and feel torn between their parents. This can lead to behavioral issues, as children struggle to navigate the conflicting messages they receive. A father who experiences panic attacks due to unpredictable interactions with his ex might find it challenging to be present and engaged with his children. The constant anxiety can make it difficult to focus on their needs, creating a strained and stressful environment for everyone involved.

To illustrate the psychological toll of narcissistic abuse, consider the case of a mother who found herself constantly undermined by her narcissistic ex. Every time she made a decision about their child's upbringing, her ex would dismiss her choices and assert his own. This constant invalidation left her feeling powerless and questioning her abilities as a parent. She noticed that her children started to mimic their father's dismissive behavior, further eroding her confidence. The emotional manipulation extended to every aspect of their co-parenting relationship, leaving her feeling trapped and overwhelmed.

Initial coping mechanisms are crucial for mitigating the psychological impact of narcissistic abuse. The first step is recognizing the abuse. Acknowledging that you are being manipulated and mistreated is essential for taking back control. Once you recognize the abuse, seeking therapy or counseling can provide invaluable support. A therapist can help you develop coping strategies, rebuild your self-esteem, and navigate the complexities of co-parenting with a narcissist. Establishing a support network is equally important. Reach out to friends and family who can offer emotional support and practical advice. Joining support groups, either in person or online, can also provide a sense of community and understanding. These initial steps can help you regain a sense of control and begin the healing process.

1.3 RECOGNIZING GASLIGHTING AND MANIPULATION TACTICS

Gaslighting is a term that describes a form of psychological manipulation where the abuser seeks to sow seeds of doubt in the victim, making them question their own memory, perception, or sanity. The purpose of gaslighting is to control and destabilize the victim, creating a sense of dependency and confusion. This tactic often involves the denial of facts and the twisting of reality. For instance, a narcissistic ex might insist that an agreed-upon visitation schedule was never discussed, leaving you feeling unsure and second-guessing your own recollection of events. This persistent denial of facts can erode your confidence, making you more susceptible to further manipulation.

Another aspect of gaslighting is the twisting of reality. Narcissists are adept at reinterpreting events and conversations to suit their narrative. They might claim that you are the one being unreasonable or overly emotional, even when their behavior is clearly out of line. This tactic can make you feel as though you are losing touch with reality, causing you to doubt your judgment and instincts. Over time, this erosion of trust in your own perceptions can lead to a sense of helplessness and confusion.

Beyond gaslighting, narcissists employ various manipulation tactics to maintain control in co-parenting situations. One such tactic is triangulation, where the narcissist involves a third party to create conflict or confusion. For example, they might tell your child one thing and you another, leading to misunderstandings and tension. This tactic not only undermines your parenting but also places the child in the middle of the conflict, causing emotional distress.

Projection is another common manipulation tactic. Narcissists often accuse others of the very behaviors they themselves are guilty of. If your ex frequently accuses you of being irresponsible or neglectful, it may be a projection of their own shortcomings. This tactic shifts the focus away from their behavior and places the blame on you, further destabilizing your sense of reality. Love-bombing is a more insidious form of manipulation, where the narcissist showers you with affection and attention to regain control. They might suddenly become overly cooperative and charming, making you question whether things are really as bad as they seem. This tactic can create a cycle of hope and disappointment, making it harder to break free from their influence.

The impact of these tactics on your reality and self-worth can be profound. You might find yourself doubting your memory, feeling perpetually confused and unsure of your own perceptions. This constant state of uncertainty can erode your self-esteem, making you more vulnerable to further manipulation. For instance, you may start to believe that you are indeed the unreasonable one, as your ex claims, leading to a cycle of self-doubt and anxiety.

To counteract these manipulation tactics, it is crucial to keep detailed records of all interactions. Documenting conversations, agreements, and incidents can provide a clear and objective reference point, helping you stay grounded in reality. This practice can also serve as valuable evidence in legal proceedings, should the need arise. Setting firm boundaries is another essential strategy. Clearly defining what is acceptable and unacceptable behavior can help protect your emotional well-being and reduce the narcissist's ability to manipulate you. For example, you might set boundaries around communication, specifying that all discussions about co-parenting matters be conducted via email to ensure a written record.

Trusting your own perception is equally important. It can be challenging to maintain confidence in your judgment when faced with constant gaslighting and manipulation. However, reminding yourself that your feelings and perceptions are valid can help you regain a sense of control. Seeking support from trusted friends, family, or a therapist can also provide valuable perspective and reinforce your confidence in your reality.

1.4 HOW NARCISSISM AFFECTS PARENTING STYLES

Narcissistic parenting sharply deviates from healthy parenting, distorting traditional roles in ways that can be profoundly harmful to a child's development. Narcissistic parents operate from a place of neglect, control, and conditional love. They focus on their own needs, often at the expense of their child's well-being. This behavior is rooted in their need for admiration and control, leading them to use their children as extensions of their own ego. For example, a narcissistic parent might neglect their child's emotional needs, focusing instead on how the child's achievements reflect on them. They may offer love and approval conditionally, based on the child's ability to meet their expectations, which can vary unpredictably and be impossibly high.

On the other hand, healthy parenting is characterized by nurturing, supportive, and unconditional love. Healthy parents prioritize their child's needs and well-being, offering consistent support and guidance. They provide a stable environment where the child feels valued and understood, regardless of their achievements or failures. In this environment, love is not contingent on performance but is given freely and consistently, fostering a sense of security and self-worth in the child.

The impact of narcissistic parenting on children is profound and multifaceted. Children of narcissistic parents often develop low self-esteem, as they internalize the constant criticism and conditional love they receive. They may struggle with feelings of inadequacy and worthlessness, believing that they are only as good as their last achievement. This can lead to a perpetual cycle of seeking validation and approval, both from the narcissistic parent and from others, often at the expense of their own needs and desires.

Trust issues are another common outcome. Children learn early on that their narcissistic parent's love and approval are fickle and can be withdrawn without warning. This unpredictability can make it difficult for them to trust others, as they constantly fear rejection or criticism. These trust issues can extend into adulthood, affecting their relationships and interactions in significant ways. They may find it challenging to form close, meaningful connections, always guarded and wary of being hurt or manipulated.

Real-life examples illustrate these impacts vividly. Consider a child who feels torn between two parents. The narcissistic parent might manipulate the child into taking sides, using guilt and pressure to drive a wedge between the child and the other parent. This can leave the child feeling confused and conflicted, unsure of where their loyalty should lie. Another example is a child exhibiting behavioral issues at school. The constant emotional turmoil at home, combined with the pressure to meet the narcissistic parent's expectations, can lead to acting out, difficulty concentrating, and poor academic performance.

To mitigate these negative impacts, the non-narcissistic parent must provide consistent love and support. This means creating a stable and nurturing environment where the child feels valued and understood. Encouraging open communication is crucial. Let your child know that they can express their feelings and concerns without fear of judgment or reprisal. This open line of communication can help them process their emotions and develop a healthier sense of self-worth.

One practical way to provide consistent support is through regular routines and rituals that reinforce stability. For example, having a set bedtime routine or weekly family activities can create a sense of normalcy and security for the child. Additionally, it's essential to validate your child's feelings and experiences. Acknowledge the challenges they face with their narcissistic parents and reassure them that their feelings are valid and important.

Encouraging open communication involves actively listening to your child and providing a safe space for them to share their thoughts and feelings. This can be as simple as setting aside time each day to talk about their day and any concerns they might have. By being present and attentive, you can help your child feel heard and valued, counteracting the negative messages they receive from the narcissistic parent.

Incorporating these strategies into your parenting approach can make a significant difference in your child's emotional and psychological development. While you cannot control the behavior of the narcissistic parent, you can provide a counterbalance of love, support, and stability that helps your child navigate the complexities of their upbringing.

1.5 NARCISSISM AND THE LEGAL SYSTEM: WHAT TO EXPECT

Navigating the legal system when co-parenting with a narcissistic ex can feel like walking through a minefield. Narcissists often use legal proceedings as a weapon, turning what should be straightforward issues into prolonged, contentious battles. One of the common issues you may face is false accusations. Narcissists are skilled at fabricating stories to paint themselves as the victim and you as the villain. These accusations can range from claims of neglect to more serious allegations like abuse. The emotional toll of constantly defending yourself against these lies can be overwhelming, leaving you feeling perpetually on edge and questioning your own reality.

Prolonged litigation is another tactic frequently employed by narcissistic ex-partners. They thrive on the chaos and control that extended legal battles bring. By dragging out court proceedings, they aim to exhaust you emotionally, financially, and physically. This not only drains your resources but also disrupts your life and that of your child. The constant back-and-forth can make it feel like there is no end in sight, keeping you trapped in a cycle of conflict and uncertainty.

Narcissists manipulate the legal system in various ways to maintain control. Filing frivolous motions is a common strategy. These motions serve no real purpose other than to create delays and complications. They might file for modifications to custody agreements without any substantial reason, just to keep you entangled in legal proceedings. This tactic not only wastes your time and money but also keeps you in a constant state of anxiety, never knowing when the next legal hurdle will appear.

Using legal proceedings to exert control is another hallmark of narcissistic behavior. They may threaten you with legal action over minor disagreements, using the court system as a tool to intimidate and dominate. This can include filing for sole custody without any justifiable cause or making baseless claims to child protective services. These actions are designed to keep you off balance and fearful, ensuring that you remain under their control.

To navigate these challenges, legal preparedness is crucial. Documenting all interactions with your ex is a vital step in protecting yourself. Keep detailed records of conversations, emails, and any incidents that occur. This documentation can serve as evidence in court, helping to counter false accusations and frivolous motions. It provides a clear, factual account of events, which can be invaluable in legal proceedings.

Working with a lawyer experienced in high-conflict cases is another key strategy. Such lawyers understand the manipulative tactics used by narcissists and can provide the specialized support you need. They can help you develop a strong legal strategy, ensuring that you are well-prepared for court. A knowledgeable lawyer can also guide you through the complexities of the legal system, providing the expertise needed to counter your ex's manipulative tactics.

Consider the case of a woman named Lisa, who faced relentless legal battles with her narcissistic ex. He frequently filed motions to modify their custody arrangement, each time citing fabricated concerns about her parenting. Lisa, feeling overwhelmed, decided to document every interaction meticulously. She kept a journal of all communications, saved emails, and recorded incidents where her ex violated their custody agreement. When they went to court, her detailed records provided a clear picture of her ex's manipulative behavior. Her lawyer, experienced in high-conflict cases, used this evidence to successfully argue against the frivolous motions, ultimately securing a stable custody arrangement for Lisa and her child.

In another instance, a father named John faced false accusations of neglect from his narcissistic ex. She filed numerous reports with child protective services, each one unfounded but stressful and time-consuming to address. John's lawyer advised him to keep a detailed log of all his interactions with his child, including notes from teachers and doctors. This evidence proved invaluable in court, demonstrating his commitment to his child's well-being and exposing his ex's baseless claims.

The legal system can be a daunting arena when dealing with a narcissistic ex. However, by documenting interactions, working with experienced legal counsel, and staying vigilant, you can navigate these challenges more effectively. Remember, you are not alone in this battle. Many have faced similar struggles and come out stronger on the other side. Your efforts to protect yourself and your child are not in vain. With the right strategies and support, you can create a more stable and secure environment, free from the constant manipulation and control of your narcissistic ex.

SETTING AND MAINTAINING BOUNDARIES

My daughter recently faced a heartbreaking situation where she was unable to speak to her children while they were in the care of her narcissistic ex. Despite numerous attempts to reach out, her calls and messages went unanswered, leaving her in a state of deep anxiety and helplessness. The ex, aware of the distress this caused, seemed to relish in exerting control by withholding communication, using the children as pawns in a cruel game of power. This incident not only strained her emotionally but also highlighted the ongoing manipulation and the lengths to which her ex would go to maintain dominance in their co-parenting relationship. It was then that she realized the necessity of setting firm boundaries. Boundaries are not just rules; they are essential lines of protection for your emotional well-being and the stability of your child's environment.

2.1 THE IMPORTANCE OF BOUNDARIES IN CO-PARENTING

Boundaries are the invisible lines that safeguard your emotional and psychological health. They define what is acceptable behavior and what is not, creating a framework within which you can interact with your narcissistic ex without feeling overwhelmed or manipulated. In the context of co-parenting, boundaries serve multiple purposes. They protect your emotional well-being by limiting the opportunities for your ex to engage in manipulative or controlling behavior. For instance, setting a boundary that all communication should be through email can prevent the emotional toll of heated verbal exchanges.

Boundaries are also crucial for maintaining healthy parent-child relationships. They create a stable environment for your child, free from the chaos and unpredictability that often accompanies interactions with a narcissistic ex. By establishing clear rules and expectations, you provide your child with a sense of security and consistency. For example, having a structured visitation schedule ensures that your child knows what to expect, reducing anxiety and confusion.

The benefits of setting boundaries extend beyond emotional protection. Well-defined boundaries can significantly reduce conflict and stress. When both parties know the limits, there is less room for misunderstandings and disputes. Knowing the limits can lead to a more peaceful co-parenting relationship, where interactions are predictable and manageable. Additionally, having clear boundaries increases your sense of control and empowerment. You are no longer at the mercy of your ex's whims and manipulations but can instead create a more balanced and respectful dynamic. This newfound control can be immensely liberating, allowing you to focus on your well-being and that of your child.

However, setting boundaries with a narcissistic ex is not without its challenges. One of the most common difficulties is the resistance and pushback you are likely to encounter. Narcissists thrive on control and may view your boundaries as a threat to their dominance. They might react with anger, manipulation, or even attempts to undermine your efforts. For instance, they may try to guilt-trip you into relaxing a boundary or accuse you of being unreasonable. This resistance can be emotionally draining and may make you question the validity of your boundaries.

Another challenge is the internal guilt and fear of confrontation that often accompanies boundary-setting. You might worry about the repercussions of enforcing boundaries, fearing that it will escalate conflicts or upset your ex. This fear can be paralyzing, making it difficult to stand firm and maintain the boundaries you have set. Recognizing that these feelings are normal and part of the process is essential. Setting boundaries is an act of self-care and protection, and it is okay to prioritize you and your child's well-being.

Real-life examples can illustrate the importance and effectiveness of boundary-setting. Take the case of Emily, a mother who struggled with her ex's constant intrusions into her personal life. He would call her multiple times a day, often late at night, to discuss trivial matters or criticize her parenting. Feeling overwhelmed, Emily decided to set a boundary that all communication would be through email and only about issues directly related to their child. Initially, her ex resisted, accusing her of being difficult and uncooperative. But Emily stood firm, reiterating her boundary each time he called. Over time, the number of calls decreased, and their interactions became more focused and less emotionally charged.

Another example is John, a father whose ex frequently showed up unannounced at his home, disrupting his routine and causing stress for their children. John set a boundary to schedule all visits and that his ex would not enter his house. He communicated this boundary clearly and consistently, even when his ex tried to push back. By maintaining this boundary, John created a more stable and peaceful environment for his children, reducing their anxiety and improving their overall well-being.

Setting boundaries is a powerful tool in co-parenting with a narcissistic ex. It requires courage and consistency, but the benefits far outweigh the challenges. Boundaries protect your emotional health, provide stability for your child, and create a more manageable and respectful co-parenting relationship. By recognizing the importance of boundaries and committing to them, you can reclaim control and create a healthier dynamic for yourself and your child.

2.2 PRACTICAL TECHNIQUES FOR SETTING FIRM BOUNDARIES

Identifying which boundaries are necessary is the first step in reclaiming control over your interactions with a narcissistic ex. Start by considering your personal limits. What forms of communication are acceptable to you? For many, limiting interactions to written forms like email or text can reduce the emotional drain of verbal confrontations. This technique records all communications and gives you time to think before responding. Think about what you need to feel safe and respected. Stipulate that your ex cannot enter your home or must give notice before coming to pick up the children. These personal boundaries are crucial for maintaining your emotional well-being.

Child-focused limits are equally important. Establish clear visitation schedules that minimize disruptions to your child's routine. Consistency is critical for children, and having a set schedule helps them know what to expect, reducing anxiety. Establish and communicate clear boundaries on how you will make decisions for your child. For example, parents must agree before making significant choices about education or healthcare. These boundaries protect your child's stability and ensure that you remain active in their upbringing.

Communicating these boundaries is the next step. Use assertive language that leaves no room for misinterpretation. For instance, instead of saying, "I think it would be better if we email," say, "From now on, all communication should be via email." Assertiveness is not about being aggressive; it's about being clear and firm. Stay calm and composed during these discussions, even if your ex tries to provoke you. Narcissists often thrive on emotional reactions, so keeping your cool can defuse potential conflicts. Avoiding emotional triggers is crucial. Stick to the facts and refrain from engaging in arguments about past issues. The goal is to establish boundaries,

not revisit old wounds.

Consistency in maintaining boundaries is vital. With consistency, boundaries gain their effectiveness. Create a boundary enforcement plan. This enforcement plan might include specific consequences for violations. For example, if your ex repeatedly shows up unannounced, make it clear that you will not engage and will call the authorities if necessary. Keeping records of boundary violations can be helpful. Documenting incidents with dates, times, and descriptions is a must. These records will reinforce your commitment to the boundaries and provide evidence should you need it for legal reasons.

As circumstances change, it's essential to evaluate and adjust your boundaries. Regularly review them to ensure they still serve your needs and those of your child. Life is dynamic, and what worked a year ago might not be effective now. Adjustments might be necessary based on new developments, such as changes in your child's schedule or your ex's behavior. If you find it challenging to navigate this alone, involving a mediator or counselor can be beneficial. These professionals can provide an objective perspective and help facilitate discussions, ensuring that boundaries remain effective and fair.

My friend Laura, for instance, initially set a boundary that her ex could not contact her directly and had to go through a co-parenting app. This tactic worked well until her ex began using the app to send passive-aggressive messages. Laura then adjusted the boundary to limit communication to essential matters only, specifying what topics were acceptable. She communicated this change assertively and consistently enforced it by ignoring non-essential messages. Over time, her ex adapted, and their interactions became less stressful.

Maintaining boundaries with a narcissistic ex is a continuous process that requires vigilance and adaptability. Each step, identifying personal and child-focused limits to clearly communicating and consistently enforcing them, is essential in creating a stable, respectful co-parenting relationship. Adjusting boundaries as needed ensures they remain relevant and effective, providing ongoing protection for you and your child. By taking these practical steps, you can regain control and foster a healthier environment for everyone involved.

2.3 USING THE GREY ROCK METHOD TO MINIMIZE CONFLICT

The Grey Rock Method is a technique designed to make you as uninteresting as possible to the narcissist. By becoming emotionally disengaged and presenting yourself as dull and unresponsive, you reduce the narcissist's opportunities to manipulate and provoke you. This method is especially effective in co-parenting scenarios where your ex thrives on generating conflict and eliciting emotional reactions from you. The goal is to provide no emotional fuel for their manipulative tactics, leading them to lose interest in engaging with you.

Implementing the Grey Rock Method involves several practical steps. First, keep all communication factual and brief. When discussing co-parenting matters, stick to the necessary details and avoid elaborating. For instance, if your ex asks about your child's school performance, a simple response like "She is doing well in her classes" suffices. Avoid providing any additional information that could spark an argument or emotional response. Another key aspect is avoiding emotional reactions. Narcissists feed off your emotions, so maintaining a calm and neutral demeanor is crucial. Do not react to provocations or attempts to incite a reaction. If your ex sends an inflammatory text, respond with a neutral, factual statement, such as "I will address this during our scheduled meeting." Neutral language is essential. Use words and phrases that are clear and unambiguous, avoiding any emotional undertones. For example, instead of saying, "I'm agitated that you didn't show up on time," say, "You were 30 minutes late for the pickup."

Specific examples can help illustrate how to respond using the Grey Rock Method. When replying to inflammatory texts or emails, keep your responses short and devoid of emotion. If your ex accuses you of being an unfit parent, a reaction like "I have noted your concerns. Let's discuss this with the mediator" keeps the focus on resolving the issue without engaging in a heated exchange. In face-to-face interactions during child exchanges, maintain a monotone voice and avoid eye contact. If your ex tries to provoke you by criticizing your parenting in front of your child, say, "I hear your concerns," and leave it at that. When dealing with manipulative questions, keep your answers straightforward. If asked, "Why are you always so difficult?" respond with, "I'm here to discuss our child's schedule, not personal matters."

Using the Grey Rock Method can be challenging, especially when managing internal emotional reactions. It's natural to feel anger or frustration when faced with manipulative behavior. To manage these emotions, practice deep breathing techniques or mindfulness exercises before and after interactions with your ex. These practices can help you stay calm and centered, reducing the likelihood of an emotional reaction. Staying consistent under pressure is another challenge. Narcissists are persistent and may intensify their efforts if they sense their usual tactics aren't working. It's important to remain steadfast in your approach, even when it feels exhausting. Remind yourself of the long-term benefits of this method and the reduced conflict it can bring.

Seeking support from friends or a therapist can help maintain the Grey Rock Method. Discuss your experiences and frustrations with trusted individuals who can offer emotional support and practical advice. A therapist, particularly one experienced in dealing with narcissistic abuse, can help you develop coping strategies and maintain your emotional health. Additionally, joining support groups for people dealing with narcissistic ex-partners can provide a sense of community and shared understanding. Hearing from others who have successfully used the Grey Rock Method can offer encouragement and insights.

Using the Grey Rock Method requires patience and resilience. It's a strategy that, over time, can diminish the narcissist's control and reduce the conflict in your co-parenting relationship. By remaining emotionally disengaged and uninteresting, you can protect your well-being and create a more stable environment for your child.

2.4 SCRIPTS AND PHRASES FOR BOUNDARY-SETTING

Setting boundaries with a narcissistic ex can be incredibly challenging. Having prepared scripts and phrases can significantly reduce the emotional labor involved. When caught off guard, it's easy to become flustered and emotional, undermining your efforts to set firm boundaries. By having prepared responses, you ensure consistency in your communication. This consistency reinforces the boundaries and makes it clear to your ex that you are serious and unwavering in your stance. Prepared scripts provide a sense of control, enabling you to navigate difficult conversations with confidence and clarity.

Limiting the frequency of communication is often necessary to maintain your emotional well-being. You can use some scripts: "For the sake of clarity and to avoid misunderstandings, let's limit our communication to email." Another example is, "I will only respond to messages between 9 AM and 5 PM on weekdays." These statements clearly define the terms of communication, reducing the likelihood of intrusive calls or texts at all hours. They set a clear framework for when and how you will communicate, making it easier to manage interactions.

Child exchanges can also be a source of tension. Setting rules can help make these interactions smoother. You might say, "For the well-being of our child, let's agree to meet at a neutral location for exchanges." Or "Please ensure you are on time for pickups and drop-offs. If you are running late, notify me at least 30 minutes before." These scripts set clear expectations for behavior during exchanges, reducing opportunities for conflict and ensuring that the focus remains on the child's well-being.

Handling unplanned requests or changes can take time and effort. When your ex makes a sudden request, having a prepared response can help you maintain control. You could say, "I need time to consider your request. I will get back to you within 24 hours." This script gives you the space to think without feeling pressured to respond immediately. Another example is, "I understand your request, but we need to stick to the agreed schedule for consistency." This response acknowledges the request but reinforces the importance of sticking to the established plan.

Adapting these scripts to your personal communication style is crucial for authenticity. While being assertive is essential, incorporating your own language can make the interaction feel more natural. For instance, if you generally speak more casually, you might say, "Hey, can we stick to email for any parenting stuff? It just makes things clearer." Adjusting the tone based on the situation also helps. A more formal tone might be appropriate in more formal settings, such as legal discussions. In contrast, a casual tone might be more fitting during everyday interactions.

Practicing these scripts can significantly boost your confidence. Role-playing with a friend or therapist can provide valuable feedback and help you refine your responses. This practice allows you to anticipate potential reactions from your ex and prepare accordingly. Rehearsing in front of a mirror can also be beneficial. It helps you get comfortable with the language and delivery, making it easier to stay composed during actual interactions. Seeing yourself deliver the scripts confidently can reinforce your sense of control and readiness.

Prepared scripts and phrases are invaluable tools in setting and maintaining boundaries with a narcissistic ex. They provide clarity, reduce emotional labor, and ensure consistency in communication. By adapting these scripts to your style and practicing them, you can navigate difficult conversations with greater ease and confidence. This approach strengthens your boundaries and empowers you to manage interactions more effectively, creating a more stable and respectful co-parenting dynamic.

2.5 DEALING WITH BOUNDARY VIOLATIONS

Recognizing violated boundaries is crucial to maintaining your emotional and psychological well-being. Boundary violations can take many forms, such as your ex ignoring agreed-upon visitation schedules, showing up unannounced at your home, or making derogatory comments about you in front of your child. These actions disrupt your sense of stability and undermine the boundaries you've worked hard to establish. The emotional impact of unresolved violations can be significant, leading to feelings of frustration, helplessness, and increased anxiety. Psychological distress can accumulate over time, making it harder to maintain your mental health and effectively co-parent.

When a boundary violation occurs, addressing it promptly and calmly is essential. Your immediate response should be to reassert the boundary without engaging in an emotional confrontation. For example, if your ex arrives unannounced, you might say, "We agreed that visits need to be scheduled by both parties. Please respect this boundary." Documenting the violation is equally important. Keep a detailed record of the incident, noting the date, time, and specifics of what occurred. This documentation can serve as evidence if the violations continue and you need to seek legal or professional support.

Managing repeated boundary violations requires a strategic approach. Start by gradually increasing the consequences for each violation. Initially, this might involve reminding your ex of the boundary and the importance of respecting it. If the violations persist, you might escalate to more formal measures, such as involving a mediator or legal counsel. Legal support can provide the authority needed to enforce boundaries, especially if your ex is uncooperative. For instance, you might seek a court order that specifies the terms of visitation and communication, making it legally binding for your ex to adhere to these boundaries.

Taking care of yourself after dealing with a boundary violation is also crucial. The emotional toll can be draining, and prioritizing self-care is essential for maintaining your resilience. Engage in activities that help you relax and recharge, whether spending time with friends, pursuing a hobby, or practicing mindfulness and meditation. Emotional support from trusted friends, family, or a therapist can provide a safe space to express your feelings and gain perspective. Remember, taking care of yourself is not a luxury; it's necessary for your well-being and ability to continue co-parenting effectively.

Consider the story of Tom, who faced repeated boundary violations from his ex regarding their agreed-upon visitation schedule. Each time his ex arrived late or unannounced, it disrupted his plans and caused stress for their child. Tom decided to document each incident meticulously, noting the impact on their child's routine and well-being. He then sought the help of a family mediator, who facilitated discussions and helped enforce the agreed boundaries. Tom involved legal counsel when the violations continued, resulting in a court order that specified clear visitation terms. This legal backing provided the structure needed to ensure compliance and reduce conflict.

In another example, Sarah struggled with her ex's habit of making derogatory comments about her in front of their child. These comments hurt Sarah and affected her child's perception of her. She decided to address this by calmly reminding her ex of the importance of respectful communication in front of their child. Sarah documented each incident and, when the behavior persisted, sought the help of a child psychologist. The psychologist provided insights into the emotional harm caused by such comments and supported Sarah in reinforcing the boundary. Over time, this approach helped reduce the frequency of derogatory remarks and improved the overall co-parenting dynamic.

Dealing with boundary violations is an ongoing process that requires vigilance, consistency, and sometimes external support. By recognizing violations promptly, responding calmly, and involving professional help when needed, you can maintain the boundaries that protect your well-being and that of your child. Prioritizing self-care ensures that you remain resilient and capable of handling the challenges that come with co-parenting a narcissistic ex. Remember, you can enforce boundaries and create a stable, respectful co-parenting relationship.

The next chapter will explore effective communication strategies to minimize conflict and enhance cooperation in your co-parenting relationship.

EFFECTIVE COMMUNICATION STRATEGIES

The first time I truly grasped the depth of my daughter's struggles in communicating with her narcissistic ex was during a heated argument that quickly spiraled out of control. Every attempt she made to discuss their child's needs ended in accusations and deflections. It became clear that traditional communication methods would not work. This chapter will help you navigate these treacherous waters, providing strategies to maintain your sanity and protect your child's well-being.

3.1 THE BASICS OF EFFECTIVE COMMUNICATION WITH A NARCISSIST

Understanding narcissistic communication styles is the foundation of effective interaction. Narcissists often use manipulation, deflection, and gaslighting to control the conversation and avoid accountability. Deflection is a common tactic where they shift the blame or topic to avoid being held responsible for their actions. For example, if you bring up their delay to a child's event, they might respond with, "Well, you weren't on time last month either," completely sidestepping the issue. This tactic frustrates you and derails the conversation, making it difficult to address the real problem.

Manipulative questioning is another tool narcissists use to provoke reactions. They might ask loaded questions designed to put you on the defensive, such as, "Why are you always so difficult to deal with?" The purpose of these questions is not to seek information but to elicit an emotional response. They gain the upper hand by provoking you, making you seem irrational or overly emotional. Recognizing these patterns can help you stay grounded and not fall into their traps.

Setting the tone for communication is crucial in managing these interactions. Maintaining a calm, neutral tone helps to avoid escalating conflicts. Narcissists can weaponize emotions, so it's important to avoid using emotional language. Stick to factual statements that are difficult to twist. Instead of saying, "I'm upset that you missed the pickup," say, "You did not arrive at the scheduled time for the pickup." This factual approach leaves little room for manipulation and keeps the focus on the issue rather than your emotional response.

Establishing rules for communication can create a more structured and less stressful environment. Limiting communication to specific platforms like email or co-parenting apps can help keep interactions organized and provide a record of all exchanges. This approach prevents misunderstandings and reduces the emotional strain of real-time conversations. Setting time boundaries for responses is also beneficial. For instance, you might agree to respond to messages within 24 hours. This time gives you the space to consider your replies carefully, reducing the likelihood of knee-jerk reactions that can escalate conflicts.

Recognizing and avoiding triggers can significantly improve the quality of your interactions. Common triggers include blame language and past grievances. Blame language, such as "You always" or "You never," can quickly escalate tensions. Instead, use "I" statements to express your concerns without assigning blame. For example, say, "I feel concerned when the schedule isn't followed," rather than, "You never follow the schedule." This subtle shift can significantly affect how your message is received.

Steering clear of past grievances is equally important. Bringing up old issues can derail the conversation and lead to a spiral of accusations and defenses. Please focus on the present problem and how to resolve it. If your ex tries to bring up past mistakes, gently steer the conversation back to the current topic. You might say, "I understand you're upset about what happened before, but let's focus on what we can do now to improve things."

By understanding these communication patterns and implementing these strategies, you can create a more manageable and less emotionally draining interaction with your narcissistic ex. It requires patience and practice, but these techniques can help you maintain your peace of mind and focus on what truly matters: your child's well-being.

Reflection Exercise: Identifying Triggers and Crafting Responses

Take a moment to reflect on your interactions with your ex. Identify the triggers that often escalate conflicts and consider how you can reframe your responses to avoid these triggers. Write down specific examples of past interactions and how you might handle them differently using the strategies discussed. This exercise can help you prepare for future conversations and build your confidence in managing difficult interactions.

3.2 IMPLEMENTING THE BIFF (BRIEF, INFORMATIVE, FRIENDLY, FIRM) METHOD

The BIFF Method, created by Bill Eddy, is invaluable for managing communication with a narcissistic ex. This method helps you keep interactions concise and focused, minimizing the opportunity for manipulation and drama. BIFF stands for Brief, Informative, Friendly, and Firm. Keeping your responses brief means focusing on the essentials and avoiding unnecessary details that could be twisted or used against you. Informative responses focus on relevant facts, steering clear of emotional language that can escalate conflicts. Maintaining a friendly tone helps to defuse tension and shows that you are cooperative, not combative. Finally, being firm in your stance ensures that your boundaries are respected and your position is clear.

To craft an effective BIFF response, start by keeping it brief. This response means eliminating any extraneous details and sticking to the core message. For instance, if your ex sends a provocative email questioning your parenting abilities, resist the urge to defend yourself in detail. Instead, a brief response like, "I understand your concerns. Our child's well-being is a priority for both of us," acknowledges their point without engaging in a back-and-forth argument. This approach reduces the emotional toll on you and limits the narcissist's ability to draw you into a conflict.

Next, ensure your response is informative. Provide only the necessary facts and avoid any emotional commentary. For example, if your ex requests a change in the visitation schedule, respond with, "The current schedule is to provide consistency for our child. Any changes should be discussed and agreed upon in advance." This response is factual and to the point, leaving little room for misinterpretation or manipulation. By focusing on the facts, you maintain control of the conversation and reduce the likelihood of it spiraling into an emotional dispute.

Maintaining a friendly tone can be challenging, especially when dealing with a provocative or hostile ex. However, it's essential to keep communication civil and reduce conflict. For instance, if your ex accuses you of being difficult, a friendly yet firm reply might be, "I appreciate your input and want to ensure we both focus on what's best for our child. Let's discuss this in our next scheduled meeting." By showing cooperation and goodwill, this response defuses potential anger and demonstrates that you are trying to collaborate, not cause conflict.

Being firm in your stance is crucial for respecting your boundaries. A firm response is necessary if your ex repeatedly tries to alter the agreed-upon schedule. You might say, "The current schedule is set and agreed upon. Any changes need to be discussed and mutually agreed upon. I am not available for changes at this time." This response is clear and assertive, leaving no room for ambiguity. It reinforces your boundaries and clarifies that deviations from the agreed terms are unacceptable without prior discussion and agreement.

Specific examples can illustrate how to use BIFF in different co-parenting scenarios. A brief and factual reply is effective when responding to accusations and blame. For example, if your ex blames you for a missed appointment, you could respond, "I understand your frustration. We missed the appointment due to unforeseen circumstances. Let's focus on rescheduling." This brief, informative, friendly, and firm response addresses the issue without getting drawn into a blame game. Similarly, when handling requests for extra visitation time, a BIFF response might be, "I understand your desire for more time. The current schedule is for consistency. We can discuss potential changes at our next meeting." This response acknowledges the request while maintaining the structure and boundaries of the current arrangement.

Implementing the BIFF method can present challenges, particularly in staying calm under provocation. Narcissists are adept at pushing buttons to elicit emotional reactions. To overcome this, practice mindfulness techniques, such as deep breathing, to remain composed. Remind yourself of the purpose of BIFF and the long-term benefits of maintaining control over your responses. Consistency with the BIFF approach is also vital. It can be tempting to revert to old communication patterns, especially when under stress. However, sticking to BIFF ensures that your interactions remain constructive and focused on your child's well-being. Rehearse potential responses and remind yourself of the principles of BIFF before engaging in communication with your ex. This preparation can help you stay on track and maintain the effectiveness of this method over time.

3.3 TEMPLATES FOR COMMON CO-PARENTING INTERACTIONS

Navigating communication with a narcissistic ex can feel like walking on eggshells. Having prepared communication templates can significantly reduce stress and ensure consistency. These templates serve as a guide, minimizing the emotional labor required to craft each message from scratch. They allow you to deliver clear and consistent messaging, making it easier to maintain your boundaries and stay focused on your child's well-being. When emotions run high, having a template to rely on can be a lifesaver, providing structure and clarity in otherwise chaotic interactions.

One of the most frequent areas where templates prove invaluable is in scheduling and logistics. For example, confirming visitation schedules can often become a battleground. A simple, clear template can make all the difference. "Hi [Ex's Name], just confirming that [Child's Name] will be with you from [Start Date/Time] to [End Date/Time] as per our agreement. Please let me know if there are any changes. Best, [Your Name]." This message is straightforward, leaving little room for misinterpretation or manipulation. Similarly, discussing travel plans can be fraught with complications. A template like, "Hi [Ex's Name], I wanted to discuss [Child's Name]'s travel plans for [Event/Trip]. We need to finalize details by [Date]. Please let me know your availability to discuss. Thanks, [Your Name]," ensures that you cover all the necessary points without getting sidetracked.

Emergencies and urgent issues require an even more delicate approach. When notifying your ex about a child's illness, it's crucial to be clear and factual. "Hi [Ex's Name], I wanted to inform you that [Child's Name] is currently unwell with [Illness]. We will follow the doctor's advice and update you on their condition. If you have any questions, please let me know. Best, [Your Name]." This template provides all the necessary information without inviting unnecessary drama. A concise message can help manage the situation calmly for emergency changes in plans. "Hi [Ex's Name], due to [Reason], there is an urgent need to adjust [Child's Name]'s schedule. Can we discuss a temporary change for [Date]? Thank you for understanding. [Your Name]."

Customizing templates to fit your specific circumstances is vital for maintaining authenticity and effectiveness. Adjust the tone and detail to match your communication style and the nature of your relationship with your ex. If you communicate more casually, you might soften the language slightly. For instance, "Hey [Ex's Name], just a heads-up, [Child's Name] isn't feeling well, and we're seeing the doctor. Will keep you posted." Incorporate phrases that resonate with your style, ensuring the message remains clear and firm while reflecting your voice. This customization makes the interaction feel more natural and less robotic, increasing the likelihood of a positive response.

By adapting these templates, you can navigate the complexities of co-parenting communication with greater ease and confidence. The structure provided by these prepared responses helps to keep interactions focused and productive, reducing the emotional toll on you and creating a more stable environment for your child.

3.4 MANAGING EMOTIONAL TRIGGERS DURING COMMUNICATION

Identifying your emotional triggers is a crucial step in managing communication with a narcissistic ex. These triggers often stem from past experiences and interactions that have left you feeling vulnerable or hurt. Common triggers include criticism and blame, as narcissists frequently use these to undermine your confidence and provoke a reaction. Reflecting on past interactions can help you identify patterns in your ex's behavior and your responses. Take note of the situations that consistently result in emotional distress. For instance, if each time your ex criticizes your parenting, you feel a surge of anger or anxiety, this is a clear indication that criticism is a significant trigger for you. By recognizing these patterns, you can prepare yourself to handle similar situations more effectively in the future.

Maintaining composure during stressful interactions is not easy, but it is essential for your well-being and the stability of co-parenting. Deep breathing exercises can be incredibly effective in helping you stay calm. When you feel your emotions rising, take a moment to breathe deeply, inhaling through your nose and exhaling through your mouth. This simple act can help to lower your heart rate and bring a sense of calm. Mindfulness techniques like focusing on the present moment are also beneficial. When you feel triggered, try to ground yourself by paying attention to your surroundings or a specific object. This technique can shift your focus from the emotional turmoil and bring clarity.

Responding to emotional provocations with neutrality can defuse potential conflicts. When faced with personal attacks or accusations, neutral responses are key. For example, if your ex says, "You're always late picking up our child," a neutral response might be, "I understand your concern. Let's stick to the schedule we agreed on." This response acknowledges the concern without becoming defensive or escalating the situation. Redirecting the conversation to the main topic can also help. If your ex tries to sidetrack the discussion with unrelated grievances, gently steer it back by saying, "Let's focus on what's best for our child right now." This statement keeps the conversation productive and reduces the opportunity for manipulation.

Building emotional resilience is a long-term strategy that can help you handle triggering communication more effectively. Regular self-reflection practices can be invaluable in this process. Take time each day to reflect on your interactions and your emotional responses. Journaling can be an excellent tool for this, allowing you to process your feelings and identify areas for improvement. Self-care routines are equally important. Engaging in activities that nourish your mind and body can help to build your emotional strength. These might include exercise, spending time in nature, or pursuing hobbies that bring you joy. By taking care of yourself, you will be able to handle the challenges of co-parenting with a narcissistic ex.

Having a support system in place is also helpful in managing emotional triggers. Trusted friends, family members, or a therapist can provide a safe space to express your feelings and gain perspective. Having someone to talk to can make a significant difference, helping you to feel supported and less isolated. They can also offer practical advice and strategies for managing difficult interactions. Remember, you do not have to navigate this alone. Seeking support is a sign of strength, not weakness.

Navigating communication with a narcissistic ex is undoubtedly challenging. However, you can create a more manageable and less stressful dynamic by identifying your triggers, maintaining composure, responding neutrally to provocations, and building emotional resilience. These strategies require practice and patience, but over time, they can help you keep your peace of mind and focus on what truly matters: providing a stable and loving environment for your child.

3.5 THE ROLE OF PARALLEL PARENTING IN REDUCING CONFLICT

Parallel parenting is a structured approach designed to minimize direct interaction between high-conflict parents while still allowing them to share custody of their children. Unlike traditional co-parenting, which involves regular communication and joint decision-making, parallel parenting minimizes direct contact and enables each parent to manage their responsibilities independently. This method is particularly effective when one or both parents display manipulative or controlling behaviors, such as those often seen in narcissistic ex-partners.

In parallel parenting, the goal is to reduce opportunities for conflict by limiting direct communication. Instead of frequent face-to-face meetings or phone calls, parents rely on written forms of communication like email or co-parenting apps. These forms will record all interactions and allow each parent to respond thoughtfully rather than impulsively. These structured communication channels can minimize misunderstandings, and the focus remains on the child's needs rather than the parents' conflicts.

Independent decision-making is another hallmark of parallel parenting. Each parent takes responsibility for day-to-day decisions when the child is in their care, without needing to consult the other parent for every minor detail. Major decisions, such as those related to education and healthcare, are still made jointly, but day-to-day activities are separate. This approach reduces the likelihood of disputes over minor issues and allows each parent to establish their own routines and rules within their households. For example, one parent might handle school drop-offs and pickups during their custodial time while the other manages extracurricular activities.

The benefits of parallel parenting in high-conflict situations are numerous. By reducing direct interaction, parents can avoid many conflicts arising from face-to-face communication. This approach creates a more stable and peaceful environment for the child, often caught in their parents' disputes. With fewer opportunities for conflict, the child can enjoy a more predictable and less stressful routine, positively impacting their emotional and psychological well-being.

Implementing parallel parenting strategies involves several actionable steps. The first is to establish separate communication channels for exchanging information. Communicate necessary details through email or co-parenting apps, ensuring you document all interactions for future reference. Establish clear rules and boundaries for each parent, outlining responsibilities and expectations for the child's care. For instance, create a detailed parenting plan specifying each parent's custodial times, decision-making responsibilities, and emergency management guidelines.

Real-life examples can illustrate how parallel parenting works effectively. Consider a case where parents need to handle school events with minimal interaction. Instead of attending the same parent-teacher conference, each parent can schedule their own meeting with the teacher. They can share written summaries of the meeting via email, ensuring that both stay informed without needing to interact directly. This approach reduces tension and allows both parents to remain involved in their child's education without conflict.

Managing holidays and special occasions separately is another effective parallel parenting strategy. For example, one parent might celebrate a child's birthday with a party on their custodial weekend, while the other parent plans a separate celebration on a different day. Parents can avoid the stress and potential conflict of joint celebrations by keeping these events independent. This approach allows the child to enjoy special occasions with each parent without being exposed to parental disputes.

Parallel parenting is not about avoiding responsibility but about creating a structured approach that minimizes conflict and focuses on the child's well-being. By setting up clear communication channels, establishing boundaries, and managing responsibilities independently, parents can create a more stable and peaceful environment for their children. This method requires cooperation and commitment from both parents but offers significant benefits in high-conflict situations, reducing stress for everyone involved.

As we move forward, the next chapter will delve into legal advice and custody tips, providing you with the tools you need to navigate the legal complexities of co-parenting with a narcissistic ex.

LEGAL ADVICE AND CUSTODY TIPS

Navigating the legal landscape of custody can feel like an overwhelming maze, especially when dealing with a narcissistic ex-partner. I remember the sleepless nights my daughter spent poring over legal documents, trying to understand what terms like "joint custody" and "sole custody" meant for her and her child. She felt lost, unsure how to advocate for her child's best interests in a complex and intimidating system. This chapter aims to demystify custody arrangements and help you understand your rights and responsibilities, providing the knowledge to approach your custody situation confidently and clearly.

4.1 UNDERSTANDING YOUR CUSTODY RIGHTS

There are four main types of child custody arrangements: legal custody, physical custody, joint custody, and sole custody. Legal custody grants a parent the authority to make significant decisions about the child's upbringing, including education, medical care, and religious instruction. This type of custody can be awarded solely to one parent or shared jointly between both parents. Joint legal custody requires parents to collaborate on these significant decisions, fostering a sense of shared responsibility. However, when one parent is deemed incapable or unfit, sole legal custody may be granted, allowing one parent to independently make all the critical decisions.

Physical custody, on the other hand, pertains to where the child lives on a day-to-day basis. Typically, the court awards one parent primary physical custody while granting the other visitation rights. Joint physical custody means the child splits their time equally between both parents' homes, which can be beneficial in maintaining strong relationships with both parents. However, this arrangement requires high cooperation and communication, which might be challenging in high-conflict situations.

Joint custody can refer to either joint legal custody, joint physical custody, or both. Parents share the decision-making responsibilities and the child's living arrangements when the courts award joint custody. This setup aims to ensure that the child maintains meaningful relationships with both parents. However, it demands a cooperative co-parenting relationship, which might be difficult to achieve with a narcissistic ex. Conversely, sole custody combines legal and physical custody in the hands of one parent. This arrangement is when one parent is deemed unfit due to reasons such as neglect, abuse, or severe conflict.

State-specific custody laws add another layer of complexity to custody arrangements. State regulations govern child custody laws and can vary significantly from one state to another. Understanding these differences is crucial for navigating your custody case effectively. Most states prioritize the "best interests of the child" in custody decisions, but the factors considered can include the child's wishes, the parent's health, and any evidence of domestic violence or child abuse. For instance, some states may emphasize maintaining stability in the child's life, while others might prioritize the relationship with both parents equally.

To navigate these state-specific laws, it's essential to familiarize yourself with local regulations. Resources such as local legal aid organizations, family law websites, and consultations with family law attorneys can provide valuable information tailored to your state. Many online resources offer summaries of state laws, helping you understand the specific guidelines and procedures in your jurisdiction. Consulting with a local attorney specializing in family law can provide personalized advice and ensure you are fully informed about your rights and responsibilities.

In any custody arrangement, understanding your rights and responsibilities is paramount. As a parent, you have the right to make decisions about your child's upbringing, including education, healthcare, and religious practices. These decisions are valid whether you share legal custody or hold it solely. Financial responsibilities are also a critical aspect of custody arrangements. Typically, the non-custodial parent is required to pay child support to help cover the costs of raising the child. This support ensures that the child has the basic needs, regardless of which parent they live with.

Visitation schedules are another crucial component of custody arrangements. These schedules outline the specific times and days the child will spend with each parent. Consistency and clarity in these schedules are essential for providing stability and predictability in the child's life. Both parents must adhere to the agreed-upon visitation times, and any changes should be communicated and agreed upon in advance. Understanding and respecting these schedules can reduce conflicts and create a more harmonious co-parenting relationship.

Navigating custody agreements requires careful attention to detail and a clear understanding of key clauses. Custody agreements typically outline the specifics of legal and physical custody, visitation schedules, decision-making responsibilities, and financial obligations. When negotiating these terms, it's essential to prioritize the child's best interests and maintain a focus on creating a stable and supportive environment. Be prepared to discuss and negotiate terms such as holiday schedules, transportation arrangements, and guidelines for making significant child welfare decisions.

Modifying custody agreements as circumstances change is also an important consideration. Life is dynamic, and situations can evolve, necessitating adjustments to the original custody arrangement. Whether it's a change in the child's needs, a parent's relocation, or any other significant life event, it's crucial to approach modifications with flexibility and a willingness to adapt. Open communication with your ex and seeking mediation or legal assistance when needed can help facilitate these changes smoothly and ensure that the custody arrangement continues to serve the child's best interests.

Navigating the legal complexities of custody can be daunting, but understanding your rights, responsibilities, and the different types of custody arrangements can empower you to advocate effectively for your child's well-being. With the right knowledge and support, you can approach your custody situation with confidence, ensuring that your child's needs are prioritized and protected.

4.2 DOCUMENTING INTERACTIONS FOR LEGAL PROTECTION

It's a harsh reality, but when co-parenting with a narcissistic ex, documentation becomes your best ally. High-conflict situations often involve manipulation and false accusations, making it crucial to create a paper trail. This paper trail serves multiple purposes. First, it provides a tangible record used in legal proceedings to substantiate your claims and protect yourself from false accusations. Secondly, it offers a form of self-validation, reassuring you that your experiences are real and not products of your imagination.

Documenting interactions with your ex can make a significant difference in high-conflict custody disputes. Emails and text messages are prime examples of what to document. These written communications can provide clear evidence of agreements, disagreements, and any manipulative behavior. Keep all communication in written form, reducing the likelihood of misunderstandings and providing a clear record of interactions. Visitation exchanges are another critical area to document. Note the times and dates of each exchange, along with any deviations from the agreed schedule. If your ex is consistently late or fails to show up, having a record of these incidents can be invaluable in court.

You should also meticulously document boundary violations. Whether your ex shows up unannounced or disregards agreed-upon rules, document each violation with as much detail as possible. Include the date, time, and a description of what happened. This information will help build a case showing a pattern of behavior that can be detrimental to both you and your child. In high-conflict situations, even seemingly minor incidents can accumulate to demonstrate a broader pattern of manipulation and disregard for the custody agreement.

Practical methods for documenting interactions are essential for creating an effective paper trail. Keeping a detailed journal is one of the most straightforward and effective ways to document interactions. Write down dates, times, and descriptions of incidents as soon as they occur. This journal can include everything from conversations and emails to instances of boundary violations. Recording detailed descriptions helps preserve the context and emotional impact of each incident, providing a comprehensive overview of the challenges you face. In addition to journaling, consider gathering and preserving evidence such as saving text messages and emails. Create folders on your computer or use a dedicated app to organize these records. The organization makes it easier to access and present evidence when needed.

When documenting, be sure to include any witnesses who can corroborate your account. If a friend or family member is present during a visitation exchange or witnesses a boundary violation, ask them to write a brief statement describing what they saw. These witness statements can add credibility to your claims and provide additional evidence to support your case. Audio recordings can also be valuable, but be mindful of the legalities in your state regarding recording conversations. In some states, you must obtain consent from both parties to record, so it's crucial to understand the laws in your jurisdiction before using this method.

Using your documented evidence effectively in legal situations requires organization and clarity. When preparing for court, organize your documentation chronologically, making it easy to follow the sequence of events. Use tabs or folders to separate different types of evidence, such as emails, text messages, and journal entries. This organization helps present a cohesive and compelling case to the judge. Working with a lawyer is essential for using your documentation effectively. Share all relevant evidence with your attorney and discuss how to present it in court. Your lawyer can help you develop a strategy that highlights the most critical pieces of evidence and demonstrates the pattern of behavior you've documented.

Presenting evidence in a clear and concise manner is crucial for making a strong impression in court. Avoid overwhelming the judge with too much information at a time. Instead, focus on the most relevant and impactful pieces of evidence. When presenting your documentation, be prepared to explain the context and significance of each piece. For example, if you're delivering a series of text messages, provide a brief overview of the situation and how these messages demonstrate a pattern of manipulation or boundary violations.

Consider creating a summary document that outlines the key points of your evidence. This summary can serve as a reference for both you and your lawyer, ensuring that you stay focused on the most critical aspects of your case. By presenting your evidence clearly and concisely, you can make a compelling argument that supports your position and protects your rights.

4.3 WORKING EFFECTIVELY WITH LAWYERS AND MEDIATORS

Navigating the legal system when dealing with a narcissistic ex requires the right legal support. Choosing a lawyer or mediator who understands your unique challenges can make a significant difference. When selecting a lawyer, ask questions that reveal their experience with high-conflict cases. Inquire about their familiarity with narcissistic personality disorder and how they handle manipulative behaviors in court. Ask for examples of similar cases they have managed and the outcomes achieved. It's also essential to gauge their communication style. It would help if you had someone who listens, understands your concerns, and explains complex legal terms in simple language.

Finding a mediator experienced in high-conflict cases is equally crucial. Mediation can be an effective tool for resolving disputes without the need for prolonged legal battles, but only if the mediator can manage the dynamics of dealing with a narcissistic ex. Look for mediators who have specific training or certification in handling high-conflict situations. They should be skilled at diffusing tension and keeping the focus on productive negotiation. Ask potential mediators about their approach to managing manipulation and ensuring that both parties have an equal voice during sessions.

Preparing for legal consultations can help you make the most out of your meetings with lawyers and mediators. Start by gathering all relevant documentation and evidence. This evidence includes any communication records, documentation of boundary violations, and any other pertinent information. Organize these documents in a logical order, making it easy for your lawyer or mediator to review. Write down key questions and concerns before the meeting. Think about what outcomes you want to achieve and any specific issues you need advice on. This preparation ensures that you cover all essential points and make efficient use of the consultation time.

Understanding the legal process and terminology can also empower you to engage more effectively with legal professionals. Familiarize yourself with common legal terms related to custody and divorce. This knowledge will help you follow discussions more easily and ask informed questions. If you come across terms or processes you don't understand, don't hesitate to ask your lawyer or mediator for clarification. They are there to help you navigate the complexities of the legal system and should be willing to explain anything that seems confusing.

Effective communication with legal professionals is essential for building a strong case. Be concise and focused during meetings. Stick to the facts and avoid getting sidetracked by emotional details irrelevant to the legal issues. Regular updates and follow-ups are also important. Keep your lawyer or mediator informed about any new developments or changes in your situation. This ongoing communication ensures that they have the most current information and can adjust their strategies as needed.

Maximizing mediation sessions requires a strategic approach. Set clear goals for what you want to achieve through mediation. Whether finalizing a custody agreement or resolving specific disputes, having defined goals helps keep the sessions focused and productive. Stay calm and composed during mediation, even when faced with provocations from your ex. Remember that the mediator is there to facilitate a constructive dialogue, and losing your temper can undermine the process. Be open to compromise while protecting your essential boundaries. Mediation often involves finding a middle ground and being willing to negotiate can lead to more favorable outcomes. However, don't compromise on crucial issues for your and your child's well-being.

Consider the story of Rachel, who faced relentless manipulation from her ex during mediation sessions. She prepared by documenting every interaction and organizing her evidence meticulously. She chose a mediator experienced in high-conflict cases who could manage the dynamics effectively. During sessions, Rachel stayed focused on her goals and remained calm, even when her ex tried to provoke her. She was open to reasonable compromises but stood firm on issues that mattered most. This approach helped her navigate the mediation process successfully and reach a fair agreement.

Another example is Mark, who initially struggled with communicating effectively with his lawyer. He often felt overwhelmed and unsure of how to present his case. After preparing thoroughly for consultations, gathering all relevant documents, and writing down his key questions, he found that his meetings became more productive. He worked closely with his lawyers, keeping them updated on new developments and seeking clarification on any confusing legal terms. This effective communication helped build a strong case, ultimately leading to a favorable custody arrangement.

Working effectively with lawyers and mediators involves careful preparation, strategic communication, and a willingness to engage in the process constructively. By choosing the right professionals, preparing thoroughly for consultations, and communicating clearly, you can navigate the legal complexities of co-parenting with a narcissistic ex more effectively. This approach strengthens your legal position and helps create a more stable and supportive environment for your child.

4.4 STRATEGIES FOR HANDLING FALSE ACCUSATIONS IN COURT

False accusations in custody battles can be a devastating blow, both legally and emotionally. When someone falsely accuses you, it can feel like your entire world turns upside down. The damage to your reputation and credibility can be immense. These accusations can make you seem untrustworthy or unfit, influencing the court's decisions regarding custody and visitation. The emotional toll is equally heavy, leading to stress, anxiety, and a constant state of defensiveness. It's like being in a perpetual state of alert, always waiting for the next false claim to drop.

Gathering and presenting evidence is your best defense against false accusations. Start by meticulously documenting all interactions with your ex. Keep a record of emails, text messages, and other communication forms. Use digital tools that timestamp these records, as they provide an unalterable record of events.

Collecting witness statements can also be invaluable. If friends, family members, or colleagues have witnessed interactions that contradict the accusations, their statements can provide additional credibility. This combined evidence can paint a clear picture of the reality, countering the false narrative presented by your ex.

Working effectively with legal professionals is crucial when defending against false accusations. Share all relevant documentation with your lawyer. The more information they have, the better they can build a strong defense strategy. Be transparent about every detail, no matter how trivial it may seem. Your lawyer needs a complete picture to counter the accusations effectively. Together, you can develop a clear defense strategy. This strategy might involve highlighting inconsistencies in the accusations, presenting evidence that contradicts your ex's claims, or demonstrating a pattern of manipulative behavior by your ex. Your lawyer can guide you on the best approach, ensuring that your defense is robust and well-supported.

During these tumultuous times, self-care is not just a luxury; it's a necessity. The stress of handling false accusations can be overwhelming, making it crucial to prioritize your mental and emotional well-being. Seeking therapy or joining support groups can provide a safe space to express your feelings and gain perspective. Talking to others who have been through similar experiences can offer comfort and practical advice. Additionally, practicing stress-relief techniques such as mindfulness, meditation, or physical exercise can help manage anxiety and maintain emotional balance. Maintaining a strong support network of friends and family is also vital. They can offer emotional support, practical help, and a sense of normalcy amidst the chaos.

Consider the real-life example of Emma, who faced numerous false accusations from her ex during their custody battle. Emma meticulously documented every interaction, saving emails and texts and even keeping a journal of her daily activities with her child. She also gathered witness statements from friends who had observed her parenting firsthand. Her lawyer effectively countered the false claims presented in court as evidence. The court recognized the pattern of manipulative behavior from Emma's ex and ruled in her favor, granting her primary custody.

In another case, James faced accusations of neglect from his ex. He worked closely with his lawyer, providing detailed records of his interactions with his child and the care he provided. His lawyer developed a defense strategy that highlighted inconsistencies in his ex's claims and presented evidence of James's consistent and loving parenting. James also sought therapy to manage the emotional stress, which helped him stay focused and composed during the court proceedings. This combination of thorough documentation, legal strategy, and self-care led to a favorable outcome, with the court dismissing the false accusations and maintaining James's custody rights.

In custody battles with a narcissistic ex, understanding your rights and effectively documenting interactions are your strongest tools. These strategies help protect your credibility and emotional well-being. As we move forward, the next chapter will focus on protecting your child's well-being, offering practical advice on how to shield them from the emotional fallout of a high-conflict co-parenting situation.

PROTECTING YOUR CHILD'S WELL-BEING

It was a quiet evening when I noticed a change in my granddaughter. Usually full of energy, she seemed withdrawn and unusually quiet. When I asked her about her day, she shrugged and mumbled something about school being "fine". My daughter later confided that her ex had berated her in front of her during a recent exchange. It was then I realized how deeply these conflicts were affecting her, manifesting in ways we hadn't anticipated. Recognizing the signs of emotional distress in children is crucial for their well-being, especially when navigating the complexities of co-parenting with a narcissistic ex.

5.1 RECOGNIZING SIGNS OF EMOTIONAL DISTRESS IN CHILDREN

Identifying behavioral changes is often the first step in recognizing emotional distress in children. Increased aggression or irritability can be a significant indicator. Your child might lash out over minor issues or display a level of anger that seems disproportionate to the situation. This aggression can be their way of expressing frustration and confusion about the turmoil in their environment. Withdrawal from social activities is another common sign. A child who once enjoyed playdates or extracurricular activities might suddenly prefer to be alone, avoiding interactions that were previously enjoyable. This withdrawal can be a coping mechanism, a way for them to retreat from the emotional chaos around them.

Changes in sleep patterns should also be on your radar. If your child starts having trouble falling asleep, wakes up frequently during the night, or begins to sleep excessively, these could be signs of emotional distress. Sleep disturbances often reflect internal anxiety and stress, making it difficult for them to find the rest they need. Please pay attention to any significant changes in their sleep habits, as these can provide valuable insights into their emotional state.

Emotional indicators are equally important to recognize. Frequent crying or sadness is a poignant sign that something is amiss. Addressing these feelings is essential if you notice your child crying more often or appearing consistently sad. Anxiety and fearfulness are also common. Your child might seem overly worried about everyday tasks or display a heightened fear in situations that have never bothered them. This anxiety can stem from the instability and unpredictability they sense in their co-parenting environment.

Low self-esteem is another emotional indicator that warrants attention. A child experiencing emotional distress might express feelings of worthlessness or self-doubt. They might say things like, "I'm not good at anything," or "Nobody likes me." These statements reflect deeper emotional struggles and a need for reassurance and support. It's crucial to counter these feelings by providing positive reinforcement and helping them build a more positive self-image.

Emotional distress can also significantly impact a child's academic performance. A decline in grades is often one of the most noticeable signs. If your child's performance in school starts to drop, it could be a reflection of their internal struggles. Lack of concentration in school is another red flag. Teachers might report that your child seems distracted, has trouble focusing on tasks, or frequently daydreams. This lack of concentration can hinder their ability to keep up with schoolwork and participate actively in class.

Avoidance of schoolwork or attendance is also common. A distressed child might pretend to be sick to avoid going to school or outright refuse to attend. They might also need more interest in completing homework or participating in school activities. This avoidance can be a way to escape the pressures they feel at home and school. Communicating with teachers and school counselors is vital to monitor these changes and provide support.

Physical symptoms often accompany emotional distress, manifesting in ways that can cause physical illness. Headaches and stomachaches are common complaints among children experiencing stress. These symptoms can be a physical manifestation of their emotional turmoil. Frequent illness or fatigue is another indicator. Stress weakens the immune system, making your child more susceptible to illnesses. If your child is getting sick more often than usual, it is worth considering the role of stress in their overall health.

Bedwetting or regression in developmental milestones can also occur. A child who had previously outgrown bedwetting might start experiencing it again, or they might regress in other areas, such as speech or behavior. These regressions are often a sign that your child is struggling to cope with their emotions and the changes in their environment. Promptly monitoring and addressing these physical symptoms can help alleviate some of their distress.

Emotional Check-In Exercise

Regular emotional check-ins are an effective way to gauge your child's emotional state. Create a comfortable space where your child feels safe to express their feelings. Use activities like drawing or painting to help them communicate indirectly. Ask open-ended questions like, "How are you feeling today?" or "Is there something on your mind?" This exercise can provide valuable insights into their emotional world and help you identify areas where they might need additional support.

Recognizing these signs of emotional distress is crucial for providing the support and intervention your child needs. By staying attuned to their behavioral, emotional, academic, and physical changes, you can better understand their struggles and take proactive steps to protect their well-being.

5.2 CREATING A SAFE AND STABLE HOME ENVIRONMENT

Establishing consistent routines is crucial for providing your child with a sense of security and stability, especially in the midst of co-parenting conflicts. Regular mealtimes and bedtimes can offer a comforting structure that helps your child know what to expect each day. This predictability can provide comfort and reassurance, reducing anxiety and promoting a sense of normalcy. Scheduled family activities, like a weekly movie night or a Saturday morning pancake breakfast, can serve as anchors in your child's week, providing opportunities for bonding and creating positive memories.

Creating a physical and emotional safe space at home is equally important. Designate a quiet area where your child can retreat to relax and unwind. This area could be a cozy corner with soft pillows and their favorite books or a small nook where they can engage in calming activities like drawing or listening to music. Encouraging open communication without judgment is also vital. Make it clear to your child that they can talk to you about anything, and actively listen when they do. Validate their feelings and reassure them that expressing their emotions is okay. This open line of communication can help them feel safe and understood, fostering a sense of trust and security.

Positive interactions and bonding activities can strengthen your relationship with your child and provide much-needed emotional support. Family game nights or outings can be fun ways to connect and create positive experiences together. Choose activities that everyone enjoys, whether it's playing board games, going for a hike, or visiting a local museum. One-on-one time with each parent is also essential. Spend time individually with your child, focusing on activities they love. This dedicated time can help them feel special and valued, reinforcing their sense of belonging and security.

Minimizing your child's exposure to parental conflict is crucial for their emotional well-being. Using parallel parenting techniques can help reduce direct interactions with your ex, thereby limiting the chances of conflict in front of your child. Keep disagreements private and avoid discussing contentious issues in their presence. Establish clear boundaries for discussions, ensuring that any necessary conversations about co-parenting matters happen in a controlled and respectful manner. If you agree, discuss these topics only through email or during scheduled meetings, away from your child's ears. By keeping conflicts out of their immediate environment, you help maintain a peaceful and stable atmosphere at home.

Reflection Exercise: Identifying Safe Spaces and Routines

Take a moment to reflect on your current home environment. Identify areas where you can establish consistent routines and create safe spaces for your child. Write down a list of potential activities and routines that can provide structure and comfort. Consider any changes you need to minimize exposure to conflict and promote positive interactions. This exercise can help you create a more supportive and stable environment for your child, enhancing their sense of security and well-being.

5.3 SUPPORTING YOUR CHILD'S EMOTIONAL HEALTH

Encouraging your child to express their emotions freely is vital for their emotional health. Children often struggle to articulate their feelings, making it crucial to provide age-appropriate ways for them to express themselves. For younger children, art or play therapy techniques can be particularly effective. Drawing, painting, or engaging in imaginative play allows them to communicate their inner world in a non-verbal manner. These activities can serve as a window into their emotions, revealing fears, anxieties, or frustrations they might not be able to put into words. For older children, journaling or creative writing can be powerful tools for self-expression. Please encourage them to write about their day and feelings or create stories reflecting their emotions. This practice helps them process their emotions and build their emotional literacy, making it easier to identify and articulate their feelings in the future.

Teaching practical coping skills is another essential aspect of supporting your child's emotional health. Deep breathing exercises can be a simple yet effective way for children to manage their emotions. Teach them to take slow, deep breaths, inhaling through the nose and exhaling through the mouth. This technique can help calm their nervous system, reducing feelings of anxiety and stress. Positive self-talk is another valuable skill. Encourage your child to replace negative thoughts with positive affirmations. For example, if they say, "I can't do this," guide them to reframe it as "I can try my best." This shift in mindset can boost their confidence and resilience, helping them navigate challenging situations more effectively.

Sometimes, despite your best efforts, professional help may be necessary to support your child's emotional health. Knowing when to seek professional help is crucial. Signs that indicate the need for therapy include:

- Persistent sadness.
- Withdrawal from activities they once enjoyed.
- Changes in appetite or sleep patterns.
- Any signs of self-harm or thoughts of suicide.

If you notice these signs, find a child psychologist or counselor who can provide your child with the specialized support they need. A professional can offer therapeutic techniques tailored to your child's needs, helping them develop healthier coping mechanisms and emotional resilience. Consulting with your child's school counselor can also be a good starting point, as they can provide recommendations and referrals to trusted professionals.

Modeling healthy emotional behavior as a parent is one of the most impactful ways to support your child's emotional health. Demonstrating self-care practices shows your child that caring for one's emotional and physical well-being is essential. Engage in activities that recharge you, whether reading, exercising, or spending time with friends. When your child sees you prioritizing self-care, they learn to value and incorporate it into their lives. Showing empathy and understanding in your interactions with your child reinforces the importance of these qualities. Listen to your child when they share their feelings, validate their experiences, and offer comfort and support. This empathetic approach fosters a secure attachment, making your child feel seen and valued.

Managing stress in healthy ways is another crucial aspect of modeling emotional health. Children often mirror their parents' behavior, so how you handle stress can significantly influence their coping strategies. Practice stress-relief techniques such as mindfulness, meditation, or physical exercise. When faced with stressful situations, verbalize your coping strategies. For example, you might say, "I'm feeling stressed, so I'm going to take a walk to clear my mind." This transparency normalizes stress and provides practical examples of healthy coping mechanisms for your child. Please encourage them to join you in these activities, turning them into shared experiences that promote both physical and emotional well-being.

Supporting your child's emotional health requires a multifaceted approach that includes encouraging emotional expression, teaching coping skills, seeking professional help when needed, and modeling healthy emotional behavior. By providing a nurturing and supportive environment, you can help your child develop the resilience and emotional intelligence they need to navigate the complexities of life.

5.4 EDUCATING YOUR CHILD ABOUT NARCISSISTIC BEHAVIORS

Explaining narcissistic behaviors to children requires age-appropriate language and examples. For younger children, it's crucial to simplify complex concepts. You can describe a narcissistic parent as someone who sometimes behaves selfishly or doesn't always think about others' feelings. Use simple, relatable scenarios, like, "Sometimes, Mom/Dad might say things that make you feel sad or ignored. It's not because of anything you did; it's just how they are." Younger kids understand better when you frame the explanation in terms they encounter daily. For older children, you can introduce more nuanced explanations. For instance, you might say, "Narcissism is when someone needs a lot of attention and doesn't always consider how their actions affect others." Comparing it to a friend who always wants to be the center of attention, relatable examples can make the concept more understandable.

Empowering children through knowledge is a powerful step in helping them navigate interactions with a narcissistic parent. When children recognize manipulation tactics, they can better protect their emotional well-being. Teach them to identify behaviors like guilt-tripping or excessive criticism. Explain that these tactics are ways for the narcissistic parent to control the situation and that it's okay to feel upset or confused by them. Encourage children to set their boundaries. For example, if a parent constantly interrupts, teach them to say, "I need a moment to finish speaking." This encouragement empowers them to assert their needs respectfully and confidently. Understanding these dynamics helps children feel more in control and less vulnerable to emotional manipulation.

Reassuring and supporting your child is vital in this process. Always affirm their feelings and experiences. Let them know that it's okay to feel hurt, angry, or confused by the narcissistic behaviors they encounter. Say, "I understand it's hard when Mom/Dad says those things. It's okay to feel upset." Encouraging open dialogue about their concerns helps them feel heard and validated. Create an environment where they can express their worries without fear of judgment. Regularly check in with them, asking open-ended questions like, "How are you feeling about the time you spend with Mom/Dad?" This ongoing support reassures them that they are not alone in their experiences.

Using resources and tools can further assist in educating and supporting your child. Age-appropriate books on emotional intelligence can provide valuable insights. Books like "The Way I Feel" by Janan Cain or "My Many Colored Days" by Dr. Seuss help younger children understand and articulate their emotions. For older children, books like "Boundaries: A Guide for Teens" by June Hunt can offer practical advice on setting and maintaining boundaries. Educational videos or workshops can also be beneficial—platforms like YouTube offer animated videos that explain complex emotional concepts in an engaging and understandable way. Workshops or group therapy sessions can provide a safe space for children to learn and share their experiences with peers facing similar challenges.

One effective tool is role-playing scenarios. This interactive method allows children to practice responses to difficult situations. For example, you can role-play a scenario where the narcissistic parent criticizes them and then practice calm, assertive responses. This method builds their confidence and provides practical strategies they can use in real-life interactions. Encouraging them to think of solutions and role-play these scenarios helps them feel more prepared and less anxious about future encounters.

This proactive approach can significantly enhance their ability to cope with and manage the challenges posed by a narcissistic parent.

By providing age-appropriate explanations, empowering them with knowledge, offering ongoing reassurance and support, and utilizing useful resources, you can help your child navigate the complexities of having a narcissistic parent. This approach protects their emotional well-being and fosters resilience and self-confidence, equipping them with the tools they need to thrive despite the challenges they face.

5.5 SHIELDING CHILDREN FROM PARENTAL CONFLICT

Minimizing direct exposure to parental conflict is one of the most effective ways to protect your child's emotional well-being. One strategy to achieve this is by using written communication for contentious issues. Emails and co-parenting apps can provide a buffer, allowing you to carefully consider your responses and keep a record of all exchanges. This method not only reduces the likelihood of heated arguments but also provides documentation should any disputes arise in the future. It can be helpful to establish a rule that all discussions about sensitive topics, such as changes to the visitation schedule or financial matters, take place in writing. This method creates a formal and structured environment for communication, reducing the impulse to react emotionally.

Another practical approach is arranging child exchanges through a third party if necessary. This approach can be a trusted family member or a mutual friend willing to step in to facilitate the handover. Having a neutral third party present can diffuse tension and prevent conflicts from escalating in front of your child. If a third party isn't available, consider meeting in public places for exchanges. The presence of others often encourages more civil behavior and provides a layer of security for both you and your child.

Teaching your children basic conflict resolution skills can empower them to handle their own interactions more effectively. Start by role-playing conflict scenarios with your child. This skill can be a fun and educational activity where you act out different situations and practice resolving them together. For instance, you might play a scenario where a friend takes a toy without asking and then discusses how to handle it calmly and assertively. Encouraging problem-solving techniques is also important. Teach your child to think about possible solutions and the consequences of each option. This technique helps them navigate their conflicts and builds critical thinking skills to benefit them throughout life.

Creating a positive co-parenting plan that prioritizes the well-being of your children is crucial. Start by setting clear guidelines for interactions. Agree on consistent rules and discipline to provide your child with a stable and predictable environment. This consistency helps reduce confusion and anxiety, making it easier for your child to adapt to the co-parenting arrangement. Discuss and agree on how you will handle various aspects of parenting, from bedtime routines to rules about screen time. These guidelines can prevent misunderstandings and reduce the potential for conflict.

Seeking mediation can be highly beneficial for resolving ongoing conflicts. A trained family mediator can provide a neutral perspective and facilitate productive discussions. Finding a mediator with experience in high-conflict cases involving narcissistic behaviors can be particularly helpful. Preparing for mediation involves gathering all relevant information and clarifying your goals and concerns. Go into the sessions with an open mind, ready to listen and compromise where necessary. Implementing agreed-upon solutions from mediation can bring a sense of resolution and stability. It's essential to follow through on these agreements and continue to communicate openly about any adjustments that may be needed.

Checklist: Creating a Positive Co-Parenting Plan

- Set clear guidelines for interactions: Define acceptable behaviors and communication methods.
- Agree on consistent rules and discipline: Ensure that both households follow similar rules to provide stability.
- Discuss handling of various parenting aspects: Address routines, education, healthcare, and other critical areas.
- Seek mediation if necessary: Find a trained family mediator and prepare thoroughly for sessions.
- Implement agreed-upon solutions: Follow through on mediation agreements and maintain open communication for adjustments.

Shielding your children from parental conflict involves multiple strategies, from using written communication and involving third parties to teaching conflict resolution and developing a positive co-parenting plan. These steps help maintain a stable and supportive environment for your children, allowing them to thrive despite co-parenting challenges. In the next chapter, we will explore self-care and emotional support for co-parents, providing you with the tools to maintain your well-being while navigating the complexities of co-parenting with a narcissistic ex.

STEPHANIE BARNES
REVIEW REQUEST PAGE

The best way to find yourself is to lose yourself in the service of others.

— MAHATMA GANDHI

In giving, we have the power to change lives. Together, we can make a difference.

Would you be willing to lend a hand to someone just like you—someone navigating the challenges of co-parenting with a narcissistic ex and unsure where to turn for help?

My goal with *Effective Co-Parenting with a Narcissistic Ex* is to bring relief and hope to those facing this tough journey. But I can't do it alone.

Most readers choose books based on reviews, and that's where you come in. By leaving a review, you could help another parent find the guidance they desperately need.

It's free, takes just a minute, and your words could create a ripple effect of support. Your review could…

…help one more parent protect their child's well-being.
…help one more mom find peace and strength.
…help one more dad improve communication with his ex.
…help one more family heal and grow stronger.
…help one more person feel less alone.

Want to make a difference? Simply scan the QR code below and leave your review. Every word matters!

Review QR Code.

I wanted to personally thank you for picking up *Effective Co-Parenting with a Narcissistic Ex*. I know how challenging and emotional the co-parenting journey can be, especially when you're dealing with a difficult ex. It means so much that you're here, ready to learn, grow, and put your child's well-being first.

Once you've finished reading, I'd love to hear what you think! Your feedback is important to me and helps other parents who are going through similar experiences. Honest reviews make a big difference in helping people decide if this book could be helpful for them, too.

If the book resonated with you, or if there's anything you'd like to share about your experience, please consider leaving a quick review. It doesn't have to be lengthy—just a few words can help others find the support they need.

Thank you again for trusting me with your co-parenting journey. I'm so grateful to have you as a reader!

Warmly,
Stephanie Barnes

SELF-CARE AND EMOTIONAL SUPPORT FOR CO-PARENTS

One evening, when I came into town, I noticed that my daughter had lost a significant amount of weight, and her shoulders slumped with exhaustion. She showed me her phone, filled with daily texts from her ex, packed with confrontations and manipulative tactics. As she absentmindedly filled me in on what had been happening, she admitted that she was running on empty. The constant stress was taking a toll on her mental and physical health. This moment was a stark reminder of the importance of self-care in co-parenting, especially when dealing with a narcissistic ex.

6.1 THE IMPORTANCE OF SELF-CARE IN CO-PARENTING

Self-care is not a luxury; it is a necessity, especially when you are navigating the turbulent waters of co-parenting with a narcissistic ex. Maintaining emotional resilience is crucial. The constant manipulation and conflict can quickly drain your emotional resources, leaving you feeling battered and worn down. By prioritizing self-care, you replenish these resources, enabling you to respond to challenges with a clear mind and steady heart. Emotional resilience is your armor, protecting you from the daily onslaught of negativity and helping you maintain your sense of self-worth.

Preventing burnout and exhaustion is another critical reason to prioritize self-care. The demands of co-parenting, combined with the stress of dealing with a narcissistic ex, can lead to physical and emotional burnout. This state of exhaustion affects your health and your ability to parent effectively. By incorporating regular self-care practices, you can stave off burnout, ensuring that you have the energy and vitality to meet your responsibilities. When you are well-rested and mentally strong, you can provide stable support for your children, creating a nurturing and secure environment for them.

Self-care also plays a significant role in improving your overall mental health. The constant stress of co-parenting with a narcissistic ex can lead to anxiety, depression, and a host of other mental health issues. Regular self-care practices like exercise, meditation, and hobbies can help alleviate these symptoms, promoting a sense of well-being and balance. When your mental health is in good shape, you can handle the ups and downs of co-parenting, making decisions that are in the best interest of your children.

Neglecting self-care, on the other hand, can have serious consequences. Increased stress and anxiety are common outcomes, as the relentless demands and conflicts take a toll on your mental health. Emotional and physical exhaustion can set in, leaving you feeling like you are running on fumes. This state of depletion not only affects your well-being but also your effectiveness as a parent. When you are exhausted and stressed, your patience wears thin, and your ability to respond calmly and thoughtfully diminishes.

This type of stress can strain your relationships with your children and others, creating a ripple effect of stress and tension.

There are several myths about self-care that often prevent people from prioritizing it. One common misconception is that self-care is selfish. Taking care of yourself is one of the most selfless things you can do. Ensure you stay healthy to provide better care and support for your children. Another myth is that self-care requires a lot of time and money. While a spa day or a weekend getaway can be rejuvenating, self-care doesn't have to be elaborate or expensive. Walking, reading a book, or enjoying a cup of tea in silence are simple, incredibly effective activities. Lastly, some people believe that self-care is only for those who are struggling. In truth, self-care is for everyone. It is a proactive way to maintain your health and well-being, preventing issues before they arise.

Self-care comes in various forms, each offering unique benefits. Physical self-care, such as exercise and nutrition, helps maintain your body's strength and vitality. Regular physical activity can boost mood, increase energy levels, and improve overall health. Emotional self-care involves activities that nurture your emotional well-being, like journaling or talking to friends. These practices help you process your feelings, gain perspective, and release pent-up emotions. Social self-care focuses on maintaining healthy relationships and spending time with loved ones. Social connections provide support, reduce stress, and enhance your sense of belonging. Finally, mental self-care includes activities that stimulate your mind, such as reading, learning new skills, or engaging in creative pursuits. These activities keep your mind sharp, provide a sense of accomplishment, and offer a mental break from daily stresses.

Incorporating these different forms of self-care into your life can create a balanced and holistic approach to well-being. By prioritizing self-care, you can handle the challenges of co-parenting with resilience and grace. This commitment to self-care benefits you and creates a positive and

stable environment for your children, fostering their well-being and happiness.

6.2 MINDFULNESS EXERCISES FOR STRESS MANAGEMENT

Mindfulness is a powerful tool that can help you navigate the emotional rollercoaster of co-parenting with a narcissistic ex. At its core, mindfulness is about being fully present in the moment and acknowledging your thoughts and feelings without judgment. This practice enhances emotional regulation, making it easier to handle stressful interactions. When you're mindful, you're less likely to react impulsively, which can reduce conflicts and foster a calmer environment for you and your child. Mindfulness also reduces anxiety and stress by helping you focus on the present rather than worrying about the past or future. This focus can be a lifeline in the chaos of co-parenting. Moreover, mindfulness improves concentration, enabling you to be more effective in your daily tasks and interactions.

Integrate simple mindfulness exercises into your daily routine. One of the easiest techniques is deep breathing. Find a quiet space, close your eyes, and take slow, deep breaths. Inhale through your nose for a count of four, hold for four, and then exhale through your mouth for a count of four. Repeat this cycle several times. This practice activates the parasympathetic nervous system, promoting relaxation. Another effective exercise is body scan meditation. Lie comfortably and focus on each part of your body, starting from your toes and moving up to your head. Notice any tension or discomfort and breathe into those areas. This practice helps you become more aware of your body and release physical stress.

Mindful walking is another simple yet effective exercise. As you walk, pay attention to the sensation of your feet touching the ground, the movement of your legs, and the rhythm of your breath. This practice can be especially grounding when you feel overwhelmed. Progressive muscle relaxation is another technique that can help manage stress. Sit or lie in a comfortable position and systematically tense, then release each muscle group in your body, starting with your toes and working your way up to your head. This exercise helps release physical tension and promotes a sense of calm.

Incorporating mindfulness into your daily routine doesn't have to be time-consuming. Setting aside 5-10 minutes daily for mindfulness practice can make a significant difference. Consider using mindfulness apps like Headspace or Calm, which offer guided meditations and reminders to help you stay consistent. Practicing mindfulness during everyday activities is another way to integrate this practice into your life. For example, try mindful eating. Pay attention to your food's taste, texture, and aroma, savoring each bite. This practice enhances your enjoyment of meals and helps you stay present and focused.

Real-life examples illustrate the profound impact mindfulness can have. Take Jane, a mother of two who struggled with anxiety due to constant conflicts with her ex. She started practicing mindfulness by setting aside 10 minutes each morning for deep breathing exercises. Over time, she noticed a significant reduction in her anxiety levels. She felt more grounded and better equipped to handle stressful interactions. Another case is Mark, who found that incorporating body scan meditation into his nightly routine improved his sleep and overall well-being. This practice helped him release the physical tension accumulated throughout the day, promoting more restful sleep.

Mindfulness also improved his communication with his ex. By staying calm and focused during their interactions, he was able to respond thoughtfully rather than react impulsively. This shift reduced conflicts and created a more stable environment for their child. These real-life examples highlight the transformative power of mindfulness in managing the stress of co-parenting with a narcissistic ex. Incorporating these simple exercises into your daily routine can enhance your emotional resilience, reduce anxiety, and improve your overall well-being.

6.3 BUILDING A SUPPORT NETWORK

When you are co-parenting with a narcissistic ex, having a strong support network is not just beneficial; it is vital. The emotional support and validation from trusted individuals can make a world of difference. It would help if you had people who understand your struggles and can listen without judgment. This validation is crucial for maintaining your emotional well-being, especially when your ex constantly undermines your self-worth. A supportive network can also provide practical advice and resources. Whether it's tips on legal matters, parenting strategies, or managing stress, having access to knowledgeable and experienced people can be incredibly helpful. Moreover, opportunities for social interaction within this network can offer a much-needed break from the constant pressures of co-parenting. These interactions can be a source of joy and relaxation, helping you recharge and maintain a positive outlook.

There are various types of support networks available to you. Family and friends are often the first line of support. These are the people who know you best and can offer the most personalized advice and emotional backing. Support groups, both in-person and online, can also be invaluable. These groups provide a community of individuals who are going through similar experiences, offering empathy, shared wisdom, and a sense of belonging. Professional networks, including therapists and counselors, can provide more structured and specialized support. They can offer coping strategies, conflict resolution techniques, and emotional guidance tailored to your specific situation. Community resources such as church groups, parenting classes, and local organizations can also provide additional layers of support. These resources often offer programs and activities that can help you and your children navigate the complexities of co-parenting.

Building a strong support network requires effort and intentionality. Start by reaching out to existing contacts. Let your friends and family know what you are going through and how they can support you. Sometimes, people want to help but don't know how, so be specific about your needs. Joining local or online support groups can also expand your network. Look for groups that focus on co-parenting, narcissistic abuse, or general parenting support. These groups can provide both emotional support and practical advice. Attending community events and workshops is another great way to build your network. These events often attract like-minded individuals and can provide opportunities for learning and connection. Seeking professional guidance should also be a priority. Therapists and counselors can offer specialized support and help you develop effective coping strategies.

Effectively leveraging your support network involves being proactive and reciprocal. Don't be afraid to ask for help when you need it. Whether you need someone to watch your kids for a few hours, advice on a difficult situation, or simply a shoulder to cry on, reach out. Offering support in return strengthens these relationships. Be there for your friends and family when they need you, and show appreciation for their support. Regularly checking in with support members keeps these relationships strong and ensures that you stay connected. Utilize different members of your network for various types of support. For example, you might turn to a therapist for emotional guidance, a friend for practical advice, and a family member for childcare assistance. This approach ensures you get the most comprehensive support possible without overburdening any individual.

In building and leveraging a strong support network, you create a safety net that helps you navigate the challenges of co-parenting with resilience and confidence. This network supports you and provides a stable and nurturing environment for your children, helping them thrive amidst the complexities of your co-parenting reality.

6.4 INCORPORATING SELF-CARE INTO A BUSY SCHEDULE

Finding time for self-care amidst the chaos of co-parenting can feel like an impossible task.

However, effective time management can make a significant difference. Start by prioritizing tasks and activities. Identify what truly needs to be done and what can wait. This task will help you focus on the most important aspects of your day without feeling overwhelmed. Using planners or digital calendars can be incredibly helpful. These tools allow you to schedule your day, set reminders, and keep track of your commitments. By visualizing your day, you can allocate specific times for self-care activities, ensuring they don't get pushed aside.

Setting realistic goals and expectations is another crucial aspect of time management. Setting lofty goals is easy, only to feel discouraged when you can't meet them. Instead, break down your goals into smaller, manageable tasks. For example, instead of aiming to exercise for an hour every day, start with 15 minutes and gradually increase it. This approach makes your goals more achievable and less daunting. Delegating tasks when possible can also free up time for self-care. Don't hesitate to ask for help from friends and family, or even hire assistance for chores if feasible. Sharing responsibilities lightens your load and provides you with much-needed time to focus on yourself.

Incorporating quick self-care activities into your day can make a big difference without requiring a significant time investment. Taking a short walk during lunch breaks can provide a refreshing break, allowing you to clear your mind and get some exercise. Practicing deep breathing exercises for just five minutes can help reduce stress and center your thoughts. Listening to a favorite song or podcast while doing chores or commuting can lift your spirits and provide a mental escape. These small acts of self-care can be easily integrated into your daily routine, offering moments of relaxation and rejuvenation.

Creating a consistent self-care routine is essential for maintaining your well-being. Start by identifying your daily self-care needs. What activities make you feel relaxed and happy? Whether reading, exercising, or enjoying a quiet cup of coffee, recognize what rejuvenates you. Schedule these activities at specific times each day to ensure they become a regular part of your routine. For instance, set aside time each morning for a short meditation session or reserve a few minutes before bed for reading. Being flexible and adjusting the routine as needed is also essential. Life is unpredictable, and there will be days when your routine gets disrupted. Instead of feeling frustrated, adapt and find alternative times to fit in your self-care activities.

Balancing self-care with parenting responsibilities requires creativity and communication. Involving your children in self-care activities can be a fun and effective way to manage both. For example, you can turn exercise into a family activity, such as going for a walk or playing a sport together. This activity allows you to care for yourself and strengthens your bond with your children. Setting boundaries to protect your self-care time is crucial. Let your children know that there are certain times when you need to focus on yourself. Explain that this helps you be a better parent. Communicating the importance of self-care to your children can also foster understanding and cooperation. Teach them that taking care of oneself is essential for overall happiness and health. Doing this benefits you and sets a positive example for your child.

When you find the right balance, you fulfill your and your children's needs. Remember, self-care is not a luxury; it's a necessity. Prioritizing your well-being enables you to be the best parent you can be, creating a healthy and nurturing environment for your children.

6.5 SEEKING PROFESSIONAL HELP AND THERAPY

Recognizing when to seek professional help is crucial for maintaining your mental health while co-parenting with a narcissistic ex. Persistent feelings of sadness or anxiety that don't seem to lift are clear signs. If you find yourself struggling to get through the day, or if simple tasks become overwhelming, it's time to consider reaching out for help. If you have difficulty functioning in daily life, such as trouble concentrating at work or feeling constantly exhausted, it may indicate that you need professional assistance. Struggles with parenting responsibilities, feeling disconnected from your children, or being unable to meet their needs can further signify the need for support. Additionally, if you experience symptoms of PTSD or other mental health issues—such as flashbacks, severe mood swings, or panic attacks—professional help is essential.

Various types of professional help are available to support you through these challenges. Individual therapy offers a one-on-one setting where you can explore your feelings, develop coping strategies, and receive personalized guidance. It's a safe space to express your emotions and gain insights into your experiences. Group therapy provides a supportive environment where you can connect with others facing similar challenges. Sharing your story and hearing from others can be incredibly validating and healing. Couples counseling can be beneficial if you and your current partner need help navigating the complexities of co-parenting with a narcissistic ex. Specialized support for co-parenting issues, such as working with a family therapist or a mediator, can offer targeted strategies to improve communication and reduce conflict.

Finding the right therapist or counselor involves a few key steps. Start by researching credentials and specialties. Look for professionals with experience in dealing with narcissistic abuse, co-parenting conflicts, or any specific issues you're facing. Recommendations from trusted sources can also be invaluable. Ask friends, family, or your primary care doctor for referrals. Conducting initial consultations is another important step. Many therapists offer a free or low-cost initial session where you can discuss your needs and see if there's a good fit. During this consultation, consider compatibility and comfort level. Feeling safe and understood by your therapist is essential as you build this relationship on trust and openness.

Maximizing the benefits of therapy requires active participation. Being open and honest with your therapist is crucial. Share your thoughts, feelings, and experiences without holding back. This transparency lets your therapist fully understand your situation and provide the best possible guidance. Setting clear goals for therapy can also help. Whether you want to manage anxiety, improve co-parenting communication, or heal from past trauma, having specific objectives can give your session direction and purpose. Practicing techniques and exercises between sessions is another way to enhance the effectiveness of therapy. Your therapist may suggest mindfulness exercises, journaling, or other activities to help you cope with stress and process emotions. Make a commitment to incorporate these practices into your daily life.

Seeking feedback and making adjustments as needed is also important. Therapy is an ongoing process, and it's normal for your needs and goals to evolve over time. Regularly check in with your therapist about your progress and any new challenges you face. Be open to adjusting your approach if something isn't working. This flexibility can help you get the most out of your therapy experience and continue to grow and heal.

Incorporating professional help into your self-care routine can provide the support and tools needed to navigate the complexities of co-parenting with a narcissistic ex. Therapy offers a structured, compassionate environment where you can work through your challenges, develop resilience, and find a path to emotional well-being. By recognizing when to seek help, finding the right therapist, and actively participating in the process, you can create a foundation for continued growth and stability.

PERSONAL EMPOWERMENT AND GROWTH

One evening, as I reflected on my daughter's journey through the turbulence of co-parenting with a narcissistic ex, I realized how deeply the experience had eroded her sense of self-worth. The constant barrage of criticism and manipulation had left her doubting her abilities and questioning her value. This chapter helps you rebuild your self-esteem and reclaim your sense of self after enduring narcissistic abuse. Understanding the impact of such abuse on your self-esteem is the first step towards healing and empowerment.

7.1 REBUILDING SELF-ESTEEM AFTER NARCISSISTIC ABUSE

Narcissistic abuse is a devastating experience that can significantly damage your self-esteem. The ceaseless criticism and belittlement from a narcissistic ex can make you feel worthless and incapable. The narcissist scrutinizes and devalues every decision you make, leading you to question your judgment. This constant erosion of self-worth can leave deep scars, making it difficult to see your own value and strengths. Gaslighting, a common tactic used by narcissists, further undermines your self-worth by distorting your reality. You may find yourself doubting your memories and perceptions, feeling like you are losing your grip on reality. This manipulation can lead to a profound loss of confidence and a pervasive sense of self-doubt.

Recognizing and challenging negative self-talk is crucial for rebuilding self-esteem. Negative self-talk is the internal dialogue that reflects the critical and demeaning messages you've heard from your narcissistic ex. Common phrases might include "I'm not good enough," "I always mess things up," or "Nobody will ever love me." These thoughts, ingrained through years of abuse, can become a default mode of thinking. However, it's essential to understand that these are not truths but distortions imposed by your abuser. To challenge these negative thoughts, start by identifying them. Pay attention to your internal dialogue and write down the negative statements you catch yourself thinking. Once identified, you can begin to reframe these thoughts. For example, replace "I'm not good enough" with "I am capable and valuable." Replace "I always mess things up" with "I am learning and growing from my experiences." This process of reframing helps shift your mindset from self-criticism to self-compassion.

Incorporating affirmations and positive self-talk into your daily routine can further bolster your self-esteem. Affirmations are positive statements that challenge negative beliefs and reinforce your strengths. To create personalized affirmations, think about the qualities you value in yourself and the attributes you wish to cultivate. Write these affirmations down and repeat them daily. For example, "I am strong and resilient," "I deserve love and respect," or "I am confident in my abilities." Practicing these affirmations in front of a mirror can be particularly powerful. As you speak these words, looking into your own eyes helps internalize them, gradually replacing negative self-talk with positive reinforcement. Additionally, using affirmation apps can provide regular reminders and encouragement, helping you stay consistent in your practice.

Seeking support for self-esteem building is an essential part of the healing process. Joining support groups for survivors of narcissistic abuse can provide a sense of community and understanding. Sharing your experiences with others who have faced similar challenges can be incredibly validating and empowering. These groups offer a safe space to express your feelings, gain new perspectives, and receive encouragement. Working with a therapist who specializes in self-esteem issues can also be highly beneficial. A therapist can help you navigate the complexities of your emotions, identify underlying issues, and develop strategies for rebuilding your self-worth. They provide a professional and compassionate perspective, guiding you through the process of healing and growth.

Rebuilding self-esteem after narcissistic abuse is a journey that requires patience, compassion, and persistence. By understanding the impact of the abuse, challenging negative self-talk, incorporating affirmations, and seeking support, you can gradually reclaim your sense of self-worth and confidence. This chapter aims to provide you with the tools and guidance needed to navigate this path of healing and empowerment. Remember, you are not alone in this journey, and with each step you take, you are moving closer to a place of self-acceptance and empowerment.

Reflection Exercise: Identifying Negative Self-Talk

Instructions

1. **Identify Negative Thoughts:** Pay close attention to your internal dialogue over the next few days. Write down any negative thoughts you notice, especially those that seem automatic or repetitive.
2. **Analyze Patterns:** Review your list and look for patterns. Are there common themes? Do certain situations trigger these thoughts more than others?
3. **Reframe Negative Thoughts:** Write a positive, affirming statement for each negative thought that challenges the negativity. For example, replace "I'm not good enough" with "I am worthy and capable."
4. **Practice Daily:** Spend a few minutes each day reading your positive affirmations out loud. Consider doing this in front of a mirror to reinforce the message.
5. **Seek Support:** Share your reflections with a trusted friend, support group, or therapist. Discuss your progress and seek feedback and encouragement.

Engage in this exercise to begin dismantling the negative self-talk ingrained by narcissistic abuse and replace it with empowering positive affirmations. This practice is crucial to rebuilding your self-esteem and reclaiming your sense of self-worth.

7.2 SETTING PERSONAL GOALS FOR GROWTH

Setting personal goals is a powerful tool for personal growth and empowerment. It provides direction and purpose, giving you a sense of control over your future. When you set clear goals, you create a roadmap for your life that guides your actions and decisions. This forward-looking mindset encourages you to focus on what you can achieve rather than dwelling on past setbacks. It helps you envision a future where you are not only surviving but thriving, making incremental progress toward a better, more fulfilling life.

The SMART goals framework: Specific, Measurable, Achievable, Relevant, and Time-bound can be incredibly helpful in breaking down long-term goals into manageable steps. Start by making your goals specific. For example, instead of saying, "I want to be healthier," specify what that means for you, such as "I want to exercise three times a week." Measurable goals allow you to track your progress. You might decide to log your workouts or keep a food diary. Achievable goals are realistic and within your reach. If you haven't exercised in years, start with something manageable, like a 15-minute walk. Relevant goals should align with your broader aspirations. If your ultimate aim is to improve your overall well-being, incorporating regular exercise aligns perfectly with that goal. Finally, time-bound goals create a sense of urgency and help you stay focused. Set deadlines for each step, such as "I will have my first session by next Monday."

Creating a personal growth plan involves identifying improvement areas and setting short-term and long-term goals. Begin by reflecting on different aspects of your life, such as career, relationships, and health. What areas do you feel need attention? Once you've identified these areas, set specific goals. For instance, if you want to advance in your career, you might set a goal to complete a certification course within the next six months. Regularly review and adjust your plan as needed. Life is dynamic, and your goals may evolve over time. Periodic reviews help you stay on track and make necessary adjustments to reflect changes in your circumstances or aspirations.

Tracking your progress and celebrating your achievements are vital components of goal-setting. Using journals or digital trackers can help you monitor your progress and stay motivated. Documenting each step toward your goals provides a tangible record of your efforts and achievements. This approach can be incredibly motivating, especially when you face setbacks or obstacles. It serves as a reminder of how far you've come and what you can achieve.

Rewarding yourself for achieving milestones is equally important. Simple rewards, like a favorite activity or a small gift, can motivate you to keep pushing forward. Reflecting on your growth and the lessons you've learned along the way helps you appreciate your efforts and the progress you've made, reinforcing your commitment to continuous improvement.

For example, consider Sarah, who set a goal to improve her physical health after her divorce. She used the SMART framework to create a detailed plan, starting with achievable steps like walking 10,000 steps a day. She tracked her progress using a fitness app and celebrated each milestone, such as reaching 15,000 steps daily, with a small reward like a new book. Regularly reviewing her goals allowed her to adjust her exercise routine as her fitness level improved. This structured approach helped Sarah achieve her health goals and boosted her confidence and sense of accomplishment, empowering her to set and pursue new goals in other areas of her life.

Setting personal goals is not just about achieving specific outcomes; it's about fostering a mindset of growth and empowerment. It encourages you to take control of your life, make deliberate choices, and strive for continuous improvement. You can transform your aspirations into achievable milestones by setting clear goals, using the SMART framework, creating a comprehensive growth plan, and tracking your progress. This process empowers you to build a fulfilling life, one step at a time.

7.3 EXERCISES FOR BUILDING CONFIDENCE

You can build confidence gradually by nurturing it through daily practices. Establishing a morning routine that sets a positive tone for the day is a great starting point. Begin your day with activities that make you feel grounded and motivated. This routine might involve stretching, a short meditation session, or even a brisk walk. These activities help you start the day with a clear mind and a sense of purpose. Another powerful practice is gratitude. Take a few minutes each morning to jot down three things you are grateful for. This simple exercise shifts your focus from what's lacking to what's abundant in your life, fostering a positive and confident mindset.

Engaging in activities that bring you joy and fulfillment is also crucial. Whether reading a book, cooking, or gardening, carve out time for activities that make you feel alive and content. Visualization is another effective technique for building confidence. The mind is a powerful tool; visualizing successful outcomes can significantly boost your self-assurance. Imagine yourself succeeding in challenging situations, whether it's acing a presentation at work or handling a difficult conversation with grace. Close your eyes and picture every detail—the environment, your body language, the positive reactions of others. This practice helps you mentally rehearse success, making it feel more attainable. Creating a vision board can also be incredibly motivating. Gather images and words that represent your personal and professional goals, and arrange them on a board or digital platform. Place this vision board somewhere you can see it daily, constantly reminding you of your aspirations and potential.

Role-playing and practice are invaluable for building confidence in social and professional scenarios. Practicing assertive communication can help you feel more confident in expressing your needs and boundaries. Find a trusted friend or family member to role-play different scenarios with you. For example, practice saying no to unreasonable requests or asserting your opinion in a group setting. Rehearsing presentations or public speaking can also alleviate anxiety and build confidence. Stand in front of a mirror or record yourself while practicing. Pay attention to your posture, tone of voice, and facial expressions. Repetition and feedback are key; the more you practice, the more natural and confident you will feel.

Seeking opportunities for growth is essential for building confidence. Stepping out of your comfort zone and trying new things can be incredibly empowering. Consider taking up a new hobby or enrolling in a course that interests you. Whether learning a new language, taking a cooking class, or exploring a new sport, these activities provide a sense of accomplishment and expand your skill set. Volunteering in community activities is another excellent way to build confidence. It allows you to contribute to a cause you care about, meet new people, and develop new skills. Networking with like-minded individuals can also be beneficial. Attend local meetups, workshops, or online forums related to your interests. Engaging with a community of supportive and motivated individuals can boost your confidence and provide valuable connections and insights.

Reflection Exercise: Confidence-Building Practices

Instructions

1. **Morning Routine:** Identify three activities that help you start the day on a positive note. Incorporate these into your morning routine for the next week.
2. **Gratitude Journal:** Write down three things you are grateful for each morning. Reflect on how this practice impacts your mood and confidence.
3. **Visualization Exercise:** Spend five minutes each day visualizing a successful outcome in a challenging situation you anticipate. Focus on the details and emotions of your success.
4. **Role-Playing Scenarios:** Choose a scenario you find challenging. Role-play this scenario with a trusted friend, focusing on assertive communication. Reflect on how this practice affects your confidence.
5. **Seeking New Opportunities:** Identify one new hobby, course, or volunteering opportunity you want to pursue. Take the first step towards engaging in this activity.

By incorporating these practices into your daily routine, you can gradually build and maintain your confidence. Each exercise serves as a step towards a more empowered and self-assured you.

7.4 DEVELOPING RESILIENCE AND EMOTIONAL STRENGTH

Resilience is the ability to bounce back from adversity, adapt, and thrive despite life's challenges. It's a crucial trait that enables you to navigate the ups and downs of co-parenting with a narcissistic ex. Resilient individuals exhibit certain characteristics: they maintain a positive outlook, are adaptable, and possess a strong sense of purpose. These traits help them to recover from setbacks and continue moving forward. Resilience impacts mental health significantly. It acts as a buffer against stress, anxiety, and depression, promoting a sense of well-being and balance. Building resilience involves cultivating these traits and developing strategies to manage stress effectively.

One powerful way to build emotional strength is through self-reflection. Journaling is an excellent tool for this. By writing about past experiences and lessons learned, you better understand your emotions and reactions. Reflect on difficult times and identify the strengths that helped you cope. It may be your perseverance, problem-solving skills, or support network. Recognizing these strengths reinforces your resilience and prepares you for future challenges. Another reflective exercise is creating a list of personal strengths and how they have assisted you in difficult situations. This practice boosts your confidence and serves as a reminder of your inner resources.

Practical coping strategies are essential for building emotional resilience. Mindfulness and meditation are powerful techniques that help you stay present and manage stress. Regular mindfulness practice can calm your mind and improve your emotional regulation. You can do simple exercises like focusing on your breath or observing your thoughts without judgment anywhere and anytime. Physical activities are another effective way to reduce stress. Exercise releases endorphins, the body's natural mood lifters. Whether running, yoga, or a brisk walk, find an activity you enjoy and make it a part of your routine. Developing a support system is equally important. Surround yourself with people who understand your struggles and can offer emotional support. This network can include friends, family, support groups, and professionals like therapists. A reliable support system provides a sense of security and belonging, which is vital for emotional resilience.

Viewing setbacks as opportunities for growth is a mindset that can transform your experiences. When something goes wrong, take the time to analyze what happened and why. Reflect on the factors that contributed to the setback and consider what you could do differently next time. This analysis process turns mistakes into learning experiences, helping you grow and improve. Identify actionable steps for improvement. Maybe it's developing a new skill, seeking advice, or adjusting your approach. Taking specific actions empowers you and reinforces your ability to overcome challenges. Maintaining a positive outlook and perseverance is key. Even when things don't go as planned, keep your focus on your goals and keep moving forward.

Remember, resilience isn't about never falling; it's about getting back up every time you do. Developing resilience and emotional strength involves a combination of self-reflection, practical coping strategies, and a growth-oriented mindset. By understanding resilience and its impact on mental health, you can cultivate the traits and strategies needed to navigate the complexities of co-parenting with a narcissistic ex. Regular self-reflection through journaling and identifying personal strengths helps build emotional strength. Practical coping strategies like mindfulness, physical activities, and a robust support system provide the tools to manage stress effectively. Viewing setbacks as opportunities for growth and maintaining a positive outlook fosters a resilient mindset. Each of these elements contributes to a stronger, more adaptable you, capable of thriving despite adversity.

7.5 EMBRACING PERSONAL EMPOWERMENT

Taking responsibility for your personal growth is a transformative step. It starts with recognizing the immense power of personal choice. You are not merely a product of your environment or circumstances; you have the agency to shape your future. By acknowledging this, you reclaim control over your life. This empowerment comes from setting clear boundaries to protect your personal space and time. Boundaries are essential for maintaining your well-being and ensuring that you have the energy and focus to pursue your goals. They create a buffer that shields you from unnecessary stress and distractions, allowing you to invest in your growth and development.

Cultivating a growth mindset is another crucial aspect of personal empowerment. This mindset is about embracing challenges and viewing them as opportunities to learn and grow. When you encounter criticism, instead of feeling defeated, use it as constructive feedback to improve. Effort is a means to an end and a path to mastery. Every step you take, no matter how small, is progress. This perspective transforms setbacks into stepping stones, enabling continuous growth. It fosters resilience and adaptability, key traits for navigating life's complexities. When you adopt a growth mindset, you shift from a fixed perspective, where abilities seem static, to a dynamic view, where potential becomes limitless.

Engaging in continuous learning is vital for sustaining personal growth. Make a commitment to explore new subjects and skills regularly. This commitment could involve anything from taking a cooking class to learning a new language. Attending workshops and seminars can provide fresh insights and foster connections with like-minded individuals. These experiences broaden your horizons and equip you with the latest tools and perspectives.

Reading books and articles on personal development is another powerful way to keep growing. Literature on psychology, self-help, and other areas of interest can offer valuable knowledge and inspire you to apply new concepts to your life. This ongoing learning process nurtures curiosity and keeps you engaged with the world around you.

Celebrating personal empowerment is a meaningful way to acknowledge your progress and motivate continued growth. Reflect on your achievements and the strides you've made. Take time to appreciate your efforts and the improvements you've made. Sharing your successes with supportive friends and family can amplify your sense of accomplishment and foster a positive feedback loop. It creates a network of encouragement that propels you forward. Setting new goals for further growth ensures that you remain focused and driven. Each milestone reached is not an endpoint but a launching pad for your next set of aspirations. This cycle of setting and achieving goals keeps you in a state of perpetual growth and development.

Embracing personal empowerment means taking proactive steps to shape your life. It involves recognizing your power of choice, cultivating a growth mindset, engaging in continuous learning, and celebrating your progress. Each of these elements contributes to a stronger, more empowered you, capable of navigating challenges and seizing opportunities. As you continue to grow, you build a resilience and confidence foundation supporting a fulfilling and purposeful life.

As we wrap up this chapter, remember that personal empowerment is a continuous process. Each step you take, no matter how small, contributes to your growth and well-being. In the next chapter, we will explore positive parenting techniques, providing practical strategies to foster a nurturing and supportive environment for your child. By focusing on your growth, you improve your life and become a stronger, more effective parent.

POSITIVE PARENTING TECHNIQUES

On the day of the transition to his other parent, my grandson resists going, and my daughter offers gentle encouragement. It reminded me of how profoundly children crave stability and predictability, especially in high-conflict situations. This chapter focuses on positive parenting techniques to help you create a nurturing and secure environment for your child, even when co-parenting with a narcissistic ex.

8.1 POSITIVE PARENTING IN A HIGH-CONFLICT SITUATION

Establishing a calm and predictable environment is crucial for your child's security. Consistent daily routines can provide the structure they need amidst the unpredictability of parental conflict. Simple, regular activities like having breakfast together every morning or reading a bedtime story each night can create a comforting routine. These routines act as anchors, giving your child a sense of normalcy and stability. Moreover, creating a peaceful home atmosphere is essential. This routine can be as simple as maintaining a quiet and orderly space, free from unnecessary clutter and distractions. Soft lighting, calming music, and a designated quiet time create a serene environment where your child feels safe and relaxed.

Modeling positive behavior is another key aspect of positive parenting. Children learn by observing their parents, so it's essential to demonstrate healthy ways of managing stress. When you face a stressful situation, show your child how to handle it calmly and constructively. Take deep breaths, speak in a steady tone, and avoid reacting impulsively. Demonstrating patience and empathy in your interactions with others sets a powerful example for your child. When they see you treating others with kindness and understanding, they learn to mirror those behaviors.

For instance, if you're frustrated with a work situation, explain how you plan to address it calmly and thoughtfully. This approach teaches your child to handle challenges calmly and without placing blame.

Focusing on solutions rather than problems is a mindset that can transform your parenting approach. Instead of dwelling on conflicts or issues, shift the conversation towards finding solutions. For example, if your child is upset about a disrupted visitation schedule, focus on how to make the next visit special rather than lament the disruption. Involving your child in finding solutions to minor issues can also be empowering for them. Please encourage them to brainstorm ideas and contribute to problem-solving. This solution fosters a sense of agency and teaches them valuable conflict-resolution skills. For instance, if your child is struggling with a homework assignment, work together to find a solution, such as breaking the task into smaller, manageable parts or setting up a quiet study area.

Limiting your child's exposure to parental conflict is essential for their emotional well-being. Using separate communication channels for difficult discussions with your ex can help shield your child from conflicts. Opt for email or co-parenting apps to discuss contentious issues, keeping the tone business-like and focused on logistics. This approach reduces the likelihood of heated exchanges that your child will notice. Scheduling exchanges in neutral, public places can also relieve tension. A public setting often discourages aggressive behavior, making the exchange smoother and less stressful for everyone involved. For example, meeting at a park or a community center can provide a neutral ground that feels safe and less charged with emotional history.

Reflection Exercise: Identifying and Implementing Positive Parenting Techniques

Take a few moments to reflect on your current parenting practices. Identify areas where you can incorporate the strategies discussed in this chapter. Write down specific actions you can take to establish a calm and predictable environment, model positive behavior, focus on solutions, and limit your child's exposure to conflict. Implement these actions gradually and observe the positive changes in your child's behavior and emotional well-being. Reflect on these changes' impact on your family dynamics and continue to adjust your approach as needed. This exercise can help you stay mindful and intentional in your parenting, fostering a healthier and more supportive environment for your child.

Creating a calm and predictable environment, modeling positive behavior, focusing on solutions, and limiting exposure to conflict are practical steps you can take to improve your child's well-being amidst the challenges of co-parenting with a narcissistic ex. These techniques provide stability and security for your child and empower you to navigate this complex situation with confidence and resilience.

8.2 NURTURING EMOTIONAL INTELLIGENCE IN YOUR CHILD

Teaching your child to recognize and name their emotions can be a powerful tool in helping them navigate the complexities of life. Start with emotion cards or charts that visually represent different feelings. These can be particularly useful for younger children who might struggle to articulate their emotions. Spend time each day going through these cards, asking your child to identify how they are feeling and why. Reading books about feelings and discussing them can also be incredibly beneficial. Choose stories that explore a range of emotions and talk about the characters' experiences. Ask open-ended questions like, "How do you think this character feels?" and "What would you do in their situation?" This practice not only helps children identify their own emotions but also builds empathy.

Encouraging empathy and understanding is crucial in fostering emotional intelligence. Role-playing different scenarios can be a fun and effective way to develop this skill. Create situations where your child has to consider another person's feelings and respond appropriately. For example, you might pretend to be a friend who is sad because they lost their favorite toy. Ask your child how they would help their friend feel better. Discussing characters' feelings in stories or movies is another excellent method. Discuss the characters' emotions and motivations after watching a movie or reading a book. Ask questions like, "Why do you think they acted that way?" and "How would you feel if you were in their shoes?" This method helps children understand different perspectives and develop a deeper sense of empathy.

Developing coping skills is essential for managing emotions effectively. Teach your child simple deep breathing exercises to help them calm down when they are upset. One technique is the "balloon breath," where they imagine inflating a balloon in their belly as they inhale and slowly deflating it as they exhale. Creating a "calm down" space in your home can also be very helpful. This space should be a quiet, comfortable area where your child can go to relax and regroup. Include soothing items like soft pillows, favorite books, or sensory toys. Please encourage your child to use this space whenever they feel overwhelmed and spend time with them there, practicing calming techniques together.

Modeling emotional intelligence in your interactions with your child is the most impactful way to teach these skills. Talk openly about your own emotions and how you handle them. For instance, if you are feeling stressed, explain why and what you plan to do to manage it. This transparency helps your child see that experiencing a range of emotions is normal and that there are healthy ways to cope. Practicing active listening and validating your child's feelings is also essential. When your child expresses an emotion, please give them your full attention, make eye contact, and reflect on what they say. For example, if they say, "I'm mad because my friend didn't play with me," respond with, "I hear that you're feeling mad because your friend didn't play with you." This validation helps them feel understood and respected.

Reflection Exercise: Emotional Intelligence Practice

Take a moment to reflect on how you currently handle your child's emotions. Are there areas where you can improve in teaching them emotional intelligence? Write down specific actions you can take to help your child recognize and manage their emotions. Consider using emotion cards or books about feelings, role-playing scenarios, and creating a "calm down" space. Also, consider how to model emotional intelligence in your daily interactions. Practice active listening and validate your child's feelings regularly. Reflect on these changes' impact on your child's emotional well-being, and continue to adjust your approach as needed.

Teaching emotion recognition, fostering empathy, developing coping skills, and modeling emotional intelligence are all vital components in nurturing your child's emotional intelligence. These practices help your child navigate their own emotions and build strong, empathetic relationships with others, setting a foundation for their future well-being.

8.3 ENCOURAGING OPEN COMMUNICATION WITH YOUR CHILD

Creating an open and trusting atmosphere at home is crucial for fostering open communication with your child. Set aside regular one-on-one time with your child, even just a few minutes each day. You can spend this dedicated time doing activities your child enjoys, whether playing a game, drawing, or talking. During these moments, use open-ended questions to encourage dialogue. Instead of asking yes-or-no questions, try asking, "What was the best part of your day?" or "How did that make you feel?" This approach encourages your child to share more about their thoughts and feelings, helping you better understand their inner world.

Active listening is a skill that shows children they are heard and valued. When your child speaks, make eye contact and show genuine interest in what they're saying. Put away distractions like phones or laptops, and focus entirely on them. Reflecting on what your child says ensures they feel understood. For instance, if your child says, "I'm upset because my friend didn't play with me," you might respond, "It sounds like you felt hurt when your friend didn't want to play." This approach validates your child's feelings and encourages them to express themselves more openly in the future.

Using age-appropriate language is essential in making sure your child understands and feels comfortable communicating with you. For younger children, simplify complex concepts and use analogies they can relate to. For example, explaining a big change like moving homes can be likened to their favorite toy moving to a new play area. Encourage older children to articulate their thoughts more clearly by asking them to elaborate on their feelings and experiences. Prompt them with questions like, "Can you tell me more about why that made you feel that way?" This approach helps children develop their communication skills and express themselves more effectively.

Addressing difficult topics with sensitivity is a crucial part of maintaining open communication. Preparing for conversations about divorce or conflict involves thinking about what you want to say and how you want to say it. Be honest, but also consider your child's developmental level. For younger children, keep explanations simple and straightforward, avoiding unnecessary details that might confuse or overwhelm them. For older children, provide more context and be ready to answer their questions. Using books or resources to facilitate discussions can also be very helpful. Numerous children's books address topics like divorce, moving, or other significant life changes. Reading these together can provide a natural way to start difficult conversations and help your child feel less alone in their experiences.

Creating a home environment where your child feels safe to express their thoughts and feelings involves a combination of regular one-on-one time, active listening, age-appropriate language, and sensitive discussions about difficult topics. This approach fosters open communication and strengthens the bond between you and your child, providing them with the emotional support they need to navigate life's challenges.

8.4 TECHNIQUES FOR POSITIVE DISCIPLINE

Positive discipline focuses on teaching and guiding rather than punishing. It emphasizes respect and mutual understanding between you and your child. Unlike punitive measures, which may involve yelling or physical punishment, positive discipline aims to foster a healthy relationship built on trust and empathy. When you focus on teaching, you help your child understand the reasons behind rules and the consequences of their actions. This approach encourages them to make better choices out of understanding, not fear. For instance, instead of punishing your child for breaking a toy, you can guide them in understanding the importance of taking care of their belongings and how their actions impact others.

Implementing consistent rules and boundaries is essential for providing structure and security. A family rules chart can be an effective tool in this regard. Sit down with your child and create a chart that outlines acceptable behaviors and the consequences for not following them. Involve your child in this process to give them a sense of ownership and responsibility. Consistency is key. Make sure that the rules are applied fairly and consistently so your child knows what to expect. For example, enforce the 8 PM bedtime rule every night. Consistent boundaries help children feel secure and understand the limits within which they can operate.

Using natural and logical consequences is another important aspect of positive discipline. Natural consequences are the outcomes that happen naturally due to a child's actions. For example, if your child refuses to wear a jacket on a cold day, they will feel cold. This experience teaches them the importance of dressing appropriately without having to enforce a punishment. Logical consequences, on the other hand, are directly related to the behavior and are designed to teach responsibility. For instance, if your child makes a mess, a logical consequence would be having them clean it up. This approach helps children understand the connection between their actions and the consequences, fostering a sense of responsibility.

Encouraging positive behavior through praise and rewards can be highly effective. A reward chart for younger children can serve as a visual representation of their achievements. For instance, you can create a chart with stickers that they earn for completing tasks like brushing their teeth or doing their homework. Once they earn a certain number of stickers, they can choose a reward like a small toy or a special outing. Offering specific praise that acknowledges effort and improvement is crucial. Instead of generic praise like "Good job," try to specify what they did well. For example, "I'm proud of how you cleaned up your toys without being asked. You showed great responsibility." This type of praise reinforces the behavior you want to see and encourages your child to keep striving for improvement.

Creating an atmosphere of mutual respect and understanding is vital to positive discipline. When your child feels respected and understood, they are more likely to respect and understand you in return. This dynamic fosters a cooperative and harmonious relationship. Take the time to listen to your child's perspective and validate their feelings, even when you need to enforce rules or consequences. For example, if your child is upset about having to do their homework, acknowledge their feelings by saying, "I understand that you're tired and don't feel like doing homework right now. Let's figure out a way to make it easier." This approach shows empathy while still upholding the rules.

By focusing on teaching and guiding rather than punishing, implementing consistent rules and boundaries, using natural and logical consequences, and encouraging positive behavior through praise and rewards, you can create a positive and nurturing environment for your child. This approach helps them develop a sense of responsibility and self-discipline and strengthens your relationship, fostering a deeper connection built on mutual respect and understanding.

8.5 CREATING SPECIAL BONDING ACTIVITIES

Spending quality time with your children is one of the most effective ways to strengthen the parent-child bond. Setting aside dedicated "special time" regularly can make a significant difference. This particular time doesn't have to be complicated or expensive. It can be as simple as a weekly half-hour where you and your child engage in an activity you both enjoy. Whether playing a board game, taking a walk, or just sitting and talking, this consistent, focused time can help build a strong, trusting relationship. The key is to be fully present, putting away distractions like phones or work, and giving your child your undivided attention. This attention shows them that they are valued and important.

Engaging in activities that both you and your child enjoy can foster connection and create lasting memories. Cooking or baking together is a wonderful way to bond. Choose a recipe, gather the ingredients, and work together to create a meal or treat. This type of bond teaches valuable life skills and provides plenty of opportunities for conversation and laughter. Outdoor adventures like hiking or picnicking offer a chance to explore nature and spend time away from the distractions of daily life. Pack a simple lunch and head to a local park or nature reserve. The shared experience of discovering new trails or observing wildlife can create a sense of adventure and closeness. Creative projects such as arts and crafts are another fantastic way to bond. Set up a crafting station with supplies like paper, markers, glue, and other materials. Work on a project together, whether painting, making jewelry, or building something out of clay. The process of creating something together can be incredibly fulfilling and offers a great opportunity for conversation and collaboration.

Incorporating learning and growth into your bonding activities can be both enjoyable and beneficial. Reading together and discussing the stories can be a deeply enriching experience. Choose books that interest you and your child, and take turns reading aloud. Afterward, discuss the plot, characters, and themes. Ask questions like, "What did you think of the main character's decision?" or "How would you have handled that situation?" This approach fosters a love of reading and encourages critical thinking and empathy. Visiting museums or educational exhibits can also be a great way to bond while learning something new. Many museums offer interactive exhibits that are engaging for children. Spend the day exploring together, and take the time to discuss what you've seen and learned. This shared experience can spark curiosity and a love for learning.

Creating family traditions and rituals provides a sense of continuity and belonging that can be incredibly comforting for children. Weekly game or movie nights are a simple yet effective way to establish a regular family activity. Pick a night that works for everyone, and make it a routine. Whether playing board games, card games, or watching a favorite movie, this regular activity gives everyone something to look forward to and helps build a sense of togetherness. Annual family trips or celebrations can also become cherished traditions. Plan a yearly trip to a favorite destination, or create special celebrations for holidays and birthdays. These rituals provide a sense of stability and create lasting memories that your children will treasure.

You cannot overstate the importance of spending quality time with your children. It strengthens the bond between you and helps create a supportive and nurturing environment. You can foster a deep and meaningful connection with your child by setting aside dedicated "special time," engaging in enjoyable activities, incorporating learning and growth, and creating family traditions and rituals. This time together enhances your relationship and provides a stable and loving foundation that helps your child thrive.

SUPPORT SYSTEMS AND RESOURCES

Finding yourself in the midst of co-parenting with a narcissistic ex can feel incredibly isolating. I remember a particularly difficult time when my daughter was navigating the turbulent waters of shared custody. She felt like she was fighting a battle on multiple fronts, emotionally, legally, and personally, without any respite. During this period, she realized the importance of talking to a therapist. Her sessions provide her with a sense of community and understanding that she desperately needs. Additionally, there are other support groups available that offer practical advice and a sense of belonging.

9.1 FINDING AND JOINING SUPPORT GROUPS

Support groups are essential. When you're dealing with the manipulation and mind games that often come with co-parenting a narcissistic ex, having a safe space to share your experiences can be incredibly validating. You find emotional validation as you hear similar stories, realizing that you are not alone in your struggles. This shared experience fosters a sense of community and belonging, which can be a powerful antidote to your isolation. Furthermore, support groups offer practical advice and coping strategies from people who have walked the same path. This collective wisdom can provide new perspectives and actionable steps to help you navigate your situation more effectively.

Several types of support groups are available, catering to different needs and preferences. Local in-person support groups can offer the benefit of face-to-face interaction and the opportunity to build strong, personal connections. These groups often meet in community centers, churches, or other public venues. Online forums and social media groups provide a convenient alternative for those who may not have access to local groups or prefer the flexibility of online interaction—platforms like Facebook and Reddit host numerous groups specifically for co-parents dealing with narcissistic exes. Specialized groups for co-parenting or narcissistic abuse survivors can offer more targeted support, focusing on the unique challenges you face. Licensed therapists or peers who have lived through similar experiences might lead these groups.

Finding the right support group can seem daunting, but several resources can help you locate one that fits your needs. Start by searching online directories and community boards, which often list local support groups and their meeting times. You can also ask for recommendations from therapists or counselors who may have connections to reputable groups. Utilizing social media platforms can also be effective. Join relevant groups and participate in discussions to gauge whether the group dynamics and focus align with your desires. Don't hesitate to reach out to group administrators with any questions you may have before joining.

Once you've found a support group, maximizing its benefits by actively participating is essential. Sharing your experiences can be therapeutic for you and helpful to others in the group. Offering support and advice to fellow members fosters a reciprocal relationship, creating a supportive community environment. Attend meetings regularly to build strong connections and stay engaged with the group. Consistent participation helps you stay updated on valuable advice and resources while reinforcing a sense of belonging and support.

Reflection Exercise: Finding and Joining Support Groups

1. **Identify Your Needs:** Reflect on what kind of support you are looking for—emotional validation, practical advice, or a sense of community.
2. **Search for Groups:** Use online directories, community boards, and social media platforms to find potential support groups.
3. **Evaluate Potential Groups:** Look for groups that align with your needs and preferences. Reach out to group administrators if needed.
4. **Join and Participate:** Once you find a suitable group, join and actively participate by sharing your experiences and offering support to others.
5. **Reflect on Your Experience:** Regularly assess how the group is meeting your needs and make adjustments as necessary.

9.2 RECOMMENDED BOOKS AND ONLINE RESOURCES

Navigating the complexities of co-parenting with a narcissistic ex can feel overwhelming, but the right resources can offer guidance and support. One invaluable resource is a curated book list that provides insights and strategies tailored to your unique situation. Titles such as *You Can't Co-Parent with a Narcissist* by Chelsy Theriault delve into understanding narcissism and offer practical parallel parenting strategies. *The Parallel Parenting Solution* by Carl Knickerbocker suggests realistic approaches to eliminate conflict with difficult exes. For those dealing with the emotional toll of co-parenting, *Co-Parenting with a Narcissist* by Melanie Parker provides strategies for setting boundaries and managing interactions. These books offer practical advice and support your child's well-being and personal healing journey.

In addition to books, various websites and online articles provide practical advice and support. Websites like Verywell Mind offer comprehensive articles on narcissism and co-parenting, providing evidence-based advice and coping strategies. Blogs by experts and survivors share personal experiences, offering relatable insights and tips. Online forums, such as those on Reddit or specialized co-parenting platforms, host active discussions where you can seek advice and share your experiences with others facing similar challenges. These resources are invaluable for gaining new perspectives and finding reassurance that you are not alone in your struggles.

Educational videos and webinars are another excellent resource for continuous learning and support. YouTube channels dedicated to narcissistic abuse recovery provide visual and auditory learning, making complex concepts easier to understand. Webinars on co-parenting strategies, often hosted by psychologists or family therapists, offer interactive learning opportunities where you can ask questions and engage with experts. Online workshops focused on emotional resilience and self-care provide structured learning environments to enhance your coping skills and emotional strength.

Podcasts and audio resources are perfect for those who prefer auditory learning or have busy schedules. Podcasts on narcissism and recovery, such as *The Co-Parenting with a Narcissist* podcast, offer episodes that you can listen to on the go. Interviews with psychologists and co-parenting experts provide professional insights and practical advice. Audio courses on personal growth and empowerment, available on platforms like Audible, offer structured learning and can be a great addition to your daily routine. These resources cater to different learning preferences, ensuring that you have access to the support and information you need, regardless of your schedule or learning style.

9.3 UTILIZING COMMUNITY RESOURCES AND PROGRAMS

Local community centers can be a treasure trove of support for co-parents navigating the challenges of dealing with a narcissistic ex. These centers often offer parenting classes and workshops that provide practical skills and strategies for effective parenting. You might find sessions on managing stress, communicating effectively with your child, and understanding child development. Such classes are invaluable for gaining new insights and techniques to apply in your daily life. Additionally, many community centers host support groups and counseling services. These can offer a safe space to share your experiences, receive emotional support, and connect with others who understand your situation. Recreational activities for children, such as sports leagues, art classes, and summer camps, can provide your kids with a sense of normalcy and joy, giving them a break from the stress of co-parenting conflicts.

Non-profit organizations are another vital resource for families dealing with high-conflict co-parenting. Organizations like domestic violence shelters offer not only a safe haven but also services such as counseling and legal advice. These shelters can provide immediate support and long-term resources to help you navigate your situation. Legal aid organizations are also crucial, offering assistance with legal matters such as custody disputes and protective orders. They can guide you through the legal process, helping you understand your rights and options. Family support services, often provided by non-profits, can include everything from financial assistance to parenting classes, offering a holistic approach to support.

Government programs can offer substantial legal, financial, and emotional assistance. Child custody and visitation mediation services can facilitate more amicable arrangements, reducing the need for contentious court battles. Financial assistance programs, such as those providing help with childcare costs or emergency funds, can alleviate some of the financial burdens you might face. Mental health services offered through government programs can provide access to therapists and counselors who specialize in dealing with the psychological impacts of high-conflict co-parenting.

Accessing these resources is often straightforward, though it requires some initiative. Start by visiting your local community center and asking about their programs and services. Community boards and online directories can also be valuable tools for finding local services. Don't hesitate to contact non-profit organizations directly; many have dedicated staff to guide you through the available support options. Utilize social media and online forums to gather recommendations and reviews of these services, ensuring you find the most reputable and helpful resources available to you.

9.4 LEVERAGING TECHNOLOGY FOR EMOTIONAL SUPPORT

In today's digital age, technology offers a variety of tools to support your mental and emotional well-being as you navigate the challenges of co-parenting with a narcissistic ex. Mental health apps are a convenient way to incorporate self-care into your daily routine. Apps like Headspace and Calm provide guided meditations and mindfulness exercises that can help reduce stress and improve emotional regulation. Journaling and mood-tracking apps are also valuable, allowing you to document your feelings and track your emotional progress over time. Stress management and relaxation apps offer techniques such as progressive muscle relaxation and guided breathing exercises, which can be particularly helpful during high-stress interactions with your ex.

Online therapy platforms like BetterHelp and Talkspace offer a flexible and accessible way to receive professional support. These platforms provide video, phone, and text therapy options, allowing you to choose the format that best fits your lifestyle and comfort level. Whether you're at home or on the go, you can connect with a licensed therapist specializing in narcissistic abuse recovery. The convenience of online therapy means you can maintain regular sessions without the added stress of commuting, making it easier to prioritize your mental health.

Social media can also be a powerful tool for finding emotional support and connecting with others who understand your experiences. Joining Facebook groups for co-parents allows you to share your stories and receive advice from people who are in similar situations. Following Instagram accounts that offer inspirational content can provide daily motivation and remind you that you are not alone. Participating in Twitter chats focused on mental health and co-parenting can introduce you to new perspectives and strategies for managing your unique challenges. These online communities foster a sense of belonging and provide a platform for exchanging valuable insights and support.

Digital tools for self-care can further enhance your well-being by helping you manage various aspects of your life more effectively. Fitness apps can encourage you to stay active, which is crucial for maintaining both physical and mental health. Apps designed for organizing and managing daily tasks can help you stay on top of your responsibilities, reducing feelings of overwhelm. Digital planners and habit trackers allow you to set goals and monitor your progress, providing a sense of accomplishment and control. These tools can be particularly beneficial in creating a structured and balanced routine, making it easier to handle the demands of co-parenting.

Reflection Exercise: Integrating Technology for Emotional Support

1. **Identify Your Needs:** Determine what type of support you need—emotional, organizational, or physical.
2. **Select Relevant Apps:** Choose apps that align with your needs, such as Headspace for mindfulness or BetterHelp for therapy.
3. **Create a Routine:** Set aside time each day to use these tools, integrating them into your daily schedule.
4. **Track Your Progress:** Use journaling and habit-tracking apps to monitor your emotional and physical well-being.
5. **Engage with Online Communities:** Join social media groups and participate in discussions to build a supportive network.

9.5 BUILDING A STRONG SUPPORT NETWORK

Identifying key supportive individuals in your life is a crucial step in building a strong support network. Start by looking within your family. Who among them is empathetic and understanding?

Maybe it's a sibling who has always been your confidant, or perhaps a cousin who has a knack for listening without judgment. Close friends can also be invaluable. Consider those who consistently provide emotional support and whom you trust with your vulnerabilities. Professional contacts, such as therapists and counselors, play a unique role. They offer specialized guidance to help you navigate the complexities of co-parenting with a narcissistic ex. These professionals can provide a safe space to process your emotions and develop coping strategies.

Strengthening these relationships requires clear communication of your needs and boundaries. It's essential to let your support system know how they can help you. Be honest about what you're going through and what kind of support you need. Spending quality time together is another way to nurture these connections. Whether it's a coffee date with a friend or a family dinner, these moments of togetherness build a stronger bond. Don't forget to express gratitude and appreciation. A simple "thank you" can go a long way in reinforcing the support you receive. Let your support network know how much you value their presence in your life.

Expanding your support network may involve stepping out of your comfort zone. Join clubs, classes, or social groups that align with your interests. These support groups could be anything from a book club to a yoga class. These settings provide opportunities to meet new people and develop meaningful connections. Volunteering in the community is another excellent way to expand your network. It allows you to give back and introduces you to like-minded individuals who share your values. Attending networking events can also be beneficial. These gatherings, whether professional or personal, offer a chance to meet people who may become part of your support system.

Maintaining a strong support system requires ongoing effort. Regularly check in with your support members to see how they are doing and share updates about your life. Offering support in return is just as important as receiving it. Being there for your friends and family strengthens the reciprocal nature of your relationships. Honesty and openness about your journey are vital. Sharing your struggles and successes helps you process your experiences and deepens the connection with your support network.

9.6 PREPARING FOR FUTURE CHALLENGES

Anticipating future challenges in your co-parenting journey is crucial for maintaining stability and emotional well-being. Changes in custody arrangements are common and can arise from various factors such as changes in work schedules, relocation, or your child's evolving needs. Being prepared for these potential changes can help you navigate them with less stress. Additionally, new partners entering the co-parenting dynamic can introduce complexities. Considering how these new relationships might affect your child and the overall co-parenting arrangement is essential. Shifts in your narcissistic ex's behavior are also something to watch for. They may become more manipulative or aggressive, especially if they sense they are losing control. Recognizing these potential challenges early allows you to develop strategies to manage them effectively.

Creating a contingency plan is a proactive way to address these potential challenges. Start by identifying possible scenarios and responses. For example, if your ex decides to move to a new city, consider how this will affect the current custody arrangement and what changes you'll need to make. Establishing a support system for emergencies is also essential. This support group could involve arranging for a trusted friend or family member to assist with childcare if needed. Keeping important documents and information organized is another critical step. Ensure you have easy access to custody agreements, medical records, and contact information for your child's school and healthcare providers. This organization can save you time and stress during unforeseen events.

Building emotional resilience is vital for facing future challenges head-on. Practicing stress management techniques, such as deep breathing exercises and mindfulness, can help you stay calm and focused during difficult times. Developing healthy coping mechanisms, like regular physical activity or engaging in hobbies, provides an outlet for stress and keeps you grounded. Engaging in regular self-reflection and growth activities, such as journaling or attending workshops, helps foster personal development and emotional strength. These practices help you cope with immediate challenges and prepare you for future hurdles.

Seeking professional advice when facing significant challenges can provide you with the expertise and support you need. Consulting with a therapist or counselor can help you navigate emotional difficulties and develop effective strategies for managing your co-parenting relationship. Seeking legal advice for custody and visitation issues ensures that you understand your rights and options, helping you make informed decisions. Attending workshops or seminars on co-parenting strategies can offer new insights and practical tips that you can apply to your situation. These resources provide a wealth of knowledge and support, empowering you to handle challenges with confidence and resilience.

9.7 EMPOWERING YOURSELF THROUGH CONTINUED LEARNING

Committing to lifelong learning is one of the most empowering steps you can take in your co-parenting journey. Staying curious and open-minded allows you to adapt to new challenges and continuously seek knowledge that can enhance your life. This commitment to personal growth is not just about acquiring new skills; it's about fostering a mindset that embraces change and values self-improvement. Being open to learning allows you to discover innovative strategies to handle difficult situations, communicate more effectively, and support your child's well-being.

There are numerous educational opportunities that can aid your personal and co-parenting growth. You can tailor online courses and certifications to your specific needs, offering flexibility. Websites like Coursera and Udemy provide courses on effective communication and stress management. Workshops and seminars, whether in-person or virtual, provide interactive learning experiences where you can engage with experts and peers. Reading books and articles on personal development can provide valuable insights and practical advice. Authors like Brené Brown and Stephen Covey offer wisdom on topics like vulnerability and proactive living, which can be incredibly relevant to your co-parenting challenges.

Learning from others is another crucial aspect of continued learning. Attending support group meetings can provide firsthand insights from individuals who have faced similar struggles. Networking with other co-parents allows you to share experiences and learn new coping strategies. Participating in online forums and discussions can introduce you to diverse perspectives and solutions you might have yet to consider. These interactions can be enriching, providing both emotional support and practical advice.

Applying new knowledge to your co-parenting journey is where the real transformation happens. Implementing new strategies and techniques can improve your interactions with your ex and create a more stable environment for your child. Reflecting on the effectiveness of these new approaches helps you understand what works and what doesn't, allowing you to fine-tune your strategies. Adjusting and adapting based on feedback and experiences ensures you continually evolve and improve. This dynamic approach to learning and application keeps you resilient and prepared for any challenges that come your way.

9.8 FINAL WORDS OF ENCOURAGEMENT AND SUPPORT

Navigating the complex world of co-parenting with a narcissistic ex requires immense courage and resilience. Every day, you face challenges that test your patience and strength. Recognize the incredible grit it takes to manage these trials while striving to create a stable environment for your child. Celebrate the progress you've made, no matter how small. Each step forward, each boundary set, and each peaceful exchange is a testament to your dedication and love for your child. You are doing an extraordinary job, and your efforts are making a difference.

Know that your strength is an inspiration. You possess an inner power that fuels your ability to protect and nurture your child despite the adversity. Remember the positive impact you are making on your child's life. Your commitment to their well-being and your determination to provide a loving and secure home do not go unnoticed. Your child sees and feels your love and efforts, which will shape them into resilient and compassionate individuals. Your journey is not easy, but your perseverance is a beacon of hope and stability for your child.

Let's revisit some critical takeaways from this book. Setting and maintaining boundaries with a narcissistic ex is crucial for minimizing conflict and protecting your emotional well-being. Effective communication strategies help keep interactions focused and reduce opportunities for manipulation, such as using the BIFF method. Prioritizing self-care and seeking emotional support are vital for maintaining your mental health. Finally, embracing personal growth and empowerment enables you to navigate challenges with confidence and resilience. These principles form the foundation of a healthier co-parenting relationship and a more stable environment for your child.

As you move forward, I encourage you to take actionable steps toward improving your co-parenting situation and personal well-being. Set new goals and create a plan to achieve them. Seek additional resources and support through support groups, therapy, or educational opportunities. Commit to ongoing self-improvement and resilience. Your journey is a continuous process of growth and learning. Embrace each step with courage and determination, knowing that you have the tools and strength to overcome any challenge that comes your way. Your efforts pave the way for a brighter future for you and your child.

UTILIZING TECHNOLOGY AND TOOLS

I recall a particularly challenging period when my daughter's communication with her children was completely cut off by her narcissistic ex, who decided to use a communication tool inappropriately. It wasn't court-ordered, and he was using the app only to make himself look good. Each conversation seemed to end in confusion or conflict, leaving her emotionally drained and uncertain about the next steps. Despite this, she kept her cool and used the app as he requested. When used correctly, these digital tools can help streamline communication, reduce conflicts, and manage the complexities of shared custody with more ease and confidence. This chapter explores the best apps available for co-parenting communication, offering practical solutions to make your co-parenting journey more manageable.

10.1 BEST APPS FOR CO-PARENTING COMMUNICATION

In the realm of co-parenting, effective communication is crucial. Co-parenting apps have revolutionized how parents interact, manage schedules, and share important information. Among the most effective apps designed for co-parenting communication are OurFamilyWizard, TalkingParents, and Cozi. Each app has unique features tailored to meet the specific needs of co-parents, making them invaluable tools for managing the complexities of shared custody.

OurFamilyWizard stands out as a comprehensive co-parenting app, offering a range of features designed to facilitate smooth communication and organization. One of its most notable features is secure messaging, which ensures that all communications are tamper-proof and can be used as evidence in court if necessary. This feature alone can significantly reduce misunderstandings and conflicts, providing a clear and unalterable record of conversations. Additionally, OurFamilyWizard includes a shared calendar that allows parents to manage and view their child's schedule in real-time. This approach eliminates confusion about conflicting plans and ensures parents are on the same page with pick-ups, drop-offs, and special events. Expense tracking is another invaluable feature, enabling parents to log and share expenses related to their child, such as medical bills and extracurricular activities. Finally, the app's journaling and documentation tools allow parents to keep detailed records of important events and interactions, which can be crucial in high-conflict situations.

TalkingParents offers similar features, focusing on secure messaging, shared calendars, and expense tracking. The secure messaging function documents all communications and prevents them from being edited or deleted, providing both parents with a reliable record. The shared calendar helps manage the child's schedule, reducing the risk of double bookings and missed appointments. Expense tracking allows parents to log and share costs associated with their child, promoting transparency and fairness in financial matters. These features collectively contribute to a more organized and less contentious co-parenting relationship.

Cozi, while not specifically designed for co-parenting, has proven to be an effective tool for many families. This free app offers a color-coded shared calendar, making it easy to differentiate between various family members' schedules. Set reminders for important events to ensure you don't miss anything. Cozi also includes to-do lists and shopping lists, which can be shared between co-parents to manage everyday tasks efficiently. Although it lacks some of the advanced features of OurFamilyWizard and TalkingParents, such as secure messaging and expense tracking, Cozi remains a valuable resource for families seeking to stay organized and connected.

Setting up these apps is straightforward. For OurFamilyWizard, start by creating an account on their website or app. Once registered, you can add profiles for both co-parents and the child. These apps ensure all parties can access the necessary information and contribute to the shared calendar and expense logs. Next, set up notifications and reminders to stay informed about upcoming events and changes. This feature is handy for managing busy schedules and ensuring that both parents are aware of important dates and deadlines.

TalkingParents follows a similar setup process. Create an account and add profiles for the co-parents and child. Ensure all relevant information, such as contact details and important dates, is included. Set up notifications to receive alerts about new messages, calendar updates, and expense entries. These alerts will help you stay on top of all communications and ensure that nothing slips through the cracks.

For Cozi, download the app and create a family account. Add profiles for each family member, assigning a unique color to each person to differentiate their schedules. Input important dates and set reminders to keep everyone informed. Share to-do lists and shopping lists to manage daily tasks efficiently. Although it lacks some of the more advanced features of the other apps, Cozi's simplicity and user-friendly interface make it an excellent choice for families seeking to stay organized.

Real-life examples highlight the effectiveness of these apps in improving co-parenting relationships. One parent shared how using OurFamilyWizard's secure messaging feature significantly reduced conflicts with their ex. By having a clear and unalterable record of all communications, there was less room for misunderstandings and accusations. This parent found that their exchanges became more focused on the child's needs rather than devolving into personal attacks.

Another parent used the shared calendar feature to manage custody schedules more effectively. Previously, there needed to be more clarity about pick-up times and locations to avoid frequent conflicts and stress. Using the app's shared calendar allowed both parents to see and agree on the schedule in real time, reducing confusion and ensuring that each parent was always aware of their responsibilities. This change led to a more harmonious co-parenting relationship and a more stable environment for the child.

Cozi, though simpler, has also proved beneficial for many families. One parent shared how the app's to-do list feature helped them coordinate daily tasks with their ex. By sharing shopping lists and reminders for school events, they managed their child's needs more efficiently, reducing the need for constant back-and-forth communication. This streamlined approach allowed both parents to focus more on their children and less on logistical challenges.

You can achieve similar positive outcomes by integrating these apps into your co-parenting routine. These tools enhance communication and organization and contribute to a more stable and supportive environment for your child.

10.2 USING DIGITAL CALENDARS AND SCHEDULING TOOLS

Digital calendars have become indispensable in the realm of co-parenting, offering a centralized platform to manage schedules and reduce conflicts. When my daughter was navigating the complexities of shared custody, she found that using a digital calendar significantly streamlined her scheduling process. Centralized scheduling allows both parents to have access to the same calendar, ensuring that everyone is on the same page regarding important dates and events. This collective view eliminates the confusion of having multiple calendars and helps in avoiding double bookings. Real-time updates are another invaluable feature, enabling both parents to see changes as they happen. He immediately notes any alterations to the schedule, ensuring they are promptly visible, which reduces misunderstandings and last-minute scrambles. Moreover, digital calendars are easily accessible from various devices, allowing both parents to check and update the schedule from their phones, tablets, or computers, no matter where they are.

Among the most effective digital calendar tools for co-parenting are Google Calendar, Apple Calendar, and Microsoft Outlook. Google Calendar is a versatile and user-friendly option that offers color-coded events, which can help differentiate between various types of activities and appointments. It also integrates seamlessly with other Google services, providing a comprehensive solution for managing shared schedules. Apple Calendar, available on all Apple devices, offers similar features, including color-coded events and the ability to set reminders. Its integration with iCloud ensures that updates are synchronized across all devices, making it easy for both parents to stay informed. Microsoft Outlook, often used for professional scheduling, also offers robust calendar features suitable for co-parenting. Its shared calendar function allows both parents to view and edit events, and its integration with email and other Microsoft services provides a cohesive platform for managing both personal and professional commitments.

Setting up and integrating these digital calendars for co-parenting is straightforward. For Google Calendar, start by creating a new calendar specifically for co-parenting purposes. Share access with your ex by entering their email address and setting permissions, allowing them to view or edit events as needed. Next, set up recurring events for regular activities such as school pick-ups, extracurricular activities, and visitation schedules. This setup ensures that recurring events are automatically added to the calendar, reducing the need for constant manual updates. Finally, add reminders and notifications for important events to ensure that both parents attend significant dates and appointments.

Apple Calendar follows a similar setup process. Please create a new calendar and share it with your ex by entering their Apple ID. Set up recurring events for regular activities and add reminders to keep both parents informed. The integration with iCloud ensures that any updates are synchronized across all devices, providing real-time visibility. Microsoft Outlook also allows for the creation of shared calendars. Start by creating and sharing a new calendar with your ex and setting the appropriate permissions. Set up recurring events and add reminders to ensure that both parents are aware of important dates and activities.

Real-life scenarios illustrate the effectiveness of digital calendars in managing co-parenting schedules. One parent shared how using Google Calendar to coordinate school events significantly reduced conflicts with their ex. A shared calendar allowed both parents to see and agree on the schedule in real-time, ensuring a clear understanding of pick-up times and school activities. This collective view of the child's schedule helped parents plan their commitments around these events, providing a more stable and predictable environment for the child.

Another example highlights how shared access to a digital calendar can prevent scheduling conflicts. A parent using Apple Calendar noted that the ability to set reminders and receive notifications helped them stay on top of important dates. This proactive approach ensured that both parents were always aware of upcoming events, reducing the likelihood of missed appointments or double bookings. The real-time updates provided by the calendar allowed both parents to see any changes immediately, facilitating smoother communication and coordination.

The benefits of digital calendars extend beyond mere scheduling. They foster a sense of accountability and cooperation between co-parents. Having a shared platform where both parties can view and update the schedule leaves less room for misunderstandings or disputes. This transparency helps build trust and reduces the tension that often accompanies co-parenting arrangements. Additionally, the convenience of accessing the calendar from multiple devices ensures that both parents are always informed, no matter where they are. This accessibility is particularly valuable for parents with busy schedules, as it allows them to stay organized and engaged in their child's life.

In conclusion, integrating digital calendars into your co-parenting routine can significantly enhance communication and organization. Tools like Google Calendar, Apple Calendar, and Microsoft Outlook offer robust features that cater to the unique needs of co-parents. Setting up shared calendars, recurring events, and reminders can create a more predictable and stable environment for your child. Real-life examples demonstrate the positive impact of these tools, highlighting their potential to reduce conflicts and improve cooperation between co-parents. Embracing these digital solutions can help you navigate the complexities of co-parenting with greater ease and confidence, ultimately benefiting both you and your child.

10.3 DOCUMENTING INTERACTIONS WITH TECHNOLOGY

Documenting interactions when co-parenting with a narcissistic ex is crucial. Documentation is used for legal protection and maintaining boundaries, providing clear evidence that can be presented in court, and tracking behavior patterns. When my daughter was in the thick of her custody battles, she found that having detailed records of her interactions with her ex was invaluable. These records helped her prove instances of manipulation and inconsistency, creating a more compelling case for maintaining her child's best interests.

One key reason documentation is essential is that it provides concrete evidence in court. In high-conflict custody cases, having a clear and accurate record of communications can make a significant difference. Judges and mediators rely on factual evidence to make informed decisions, and having documented proof of interactions can help establish credibility and support your claims. Additionally, documenting interactions allows you to track patterns of behavior over time. This documentation can be vital when dealing with a narcissistic ex, as it helps to highlight instances of manipulation, gaslighting, and boundary violations. By keeping a detailed record, you can demonstrate the consistency (or lack thereof) in your ex's behavior, providing a clearer picture of the challenges you face.

Several digital tools can help with documenting interactions effectively. Evernote and OneNote are popular choices for creating and organizing digital notes. These tools allow you to set up notebooks and folders, making it easy to categorize and find specific entries. Evernote, for instance, offers features such as tagging, search functionality, and the ability to add attachments, all of which enhance your ability to keep thorough and organized records. OneNote provides similar capabilities, with the added benefit of integration with other Microsoft Office applications, making it a versatile option for documentation.

Dedicated co-parenting apps like OurFamilyWizard also come equipped with journaling features that allow you to document interactions directly within the app. These entries are time-stamped and secure, ensuring that they cannot be altered or deleted. This level of security is essential in legal contexts, where the integrity of your documentation can be critical.

Setting up these tools for effective documentation is straightforward. In Evernote, begin by creating a new notebook specifically for co-parenting interactions. Within this notebook, set up folders for different types of entries, such as emails, text messages, and in-person conversations. Add entries by copying and pasting the text or attaching screenshots, and use tags to categorize them by date, subject, or relevance. This organization makes it easy to retrieve specific information when needed. OneNote follows a similar process. Create a new notebook and set up sections for various types of interactions. Create pages for individual entries within each section, adding and organizing content as needed. Both Evernote and OneNote allow you to export your notes, which can be helpful if you need to share documentation with your lawyer or present it in court.

Dedicated co-parenting apps with journaling features simplify the documentation process even further. In OurFamilyWizard, for example, you can create journal entries directly within the app. The system automatically time-stamps and securely stores these entries, ensuring they remain unaltered. You can categorize entries by type and add notes to provide additional context. Setting up notifications for new entries can help you stay on top of your documentation, ensuring that you keep a consistent and detailed record of all interactions.

Success stories from other parents highlight the benefits of proper documentation. One parent, for instance, used Evernote to document all communications with their ex. By keeping detailed records of emails, text messages, and in-person conversations, they were able to present a comprehensive and organized account of interactions in court. This documentation helped establish a pattern of manipulative behavior by the ex, ultimately supporting their case for a more favorable custody arrangement.

Another parent found success using OneNote to keep a detailed record of custody exchanges. They documented each exchange, noting times, dates, and deviations from the agreed schedule. This thorough record-keeping proved invaluable when disputes arose about missed pick-ups and drop-offs. By presenting a clear and consistent account of these exchanges, the parent was able to demonstrate their reliability and commitment to the agreed schedule, strengthening their position in court.

Documentation not only serves as a legal safeguard but also provides emotional validation. When you are in the midst of co-parenting with a narcissistic ex, it is easy to feel gaslighted and question your perception of events. Having a detailed and organized record of interactions can help affirm your experiences and provide a sense of control. You can see patterns and recognize the manipulative tactics, empowering you to respond more effectively.

Integrating these documentation practices into your co-parenting routine can make a significant difference. By using digital tools like Evernote, OneNote, and dedicated co-parenting apps, you can keep thorough and organized records of all interactions, providing crucial evidence for legal proceedings and helping you maintain boundaries. These tools enhance your legal position and support your emotional well-being, giving clarity and validation in the face of manipulation and conflict.

10.4 LEVERAGING LEGAL TOOLS AND RESOURCES

Navigating the legal landscape of co-parenting with a narcissistic ex can be overwhelming. However, several legal tools and resources can make this process more manageable and less stressful. Custody X Change, LegalZoom, and local family law resources are among the most valuable tools available for co-parents. These resources offer a range of features that assist in creating and managing custody agreements, accessing legal forms and documents, and finding legal advice and representation.

Custody X Change is a comprehensive tool designed to help parents and legal professionals create detailed custody plans. This platform offers a variety of features, including printable calendars, parenting plan templates, expense sharing, and time tracking. One of the standout features of Custody X Change is its ability to generate legal documents from a built-in library of provisions. These documents can be printed or exported for negotiations, making the process of creating a custody agreement more straightforward and less time-consuming. The shared parenting calendars include details such as holidays, vacations, and one-time events, which can be displayed and edited on mobile devices. This flexibility ensures that both parents can access up-to-date information, reducing the likelihood of misunderstandings and conflicts.

LegalZoom provides a range of legal services, including assistance with drafting legal documents. This platform offers templates for various legal forms, such as custody agreements, visitation schedules, and child support arrangements. The design of the templates makes them easy to use, allowing you to customize them to fit your specific needs. LegalZoom also offers access to legal advice and representation through its network of attorneys. This feature is particularly beneficial for those who need professional guidance but may need more resources to hire a full-time lawyer. Using LegalZoom, you can ensure that your legal documents are accurate and comply with state laws, providing peace of mind during co-parenting.

Local family law resources are another valuable tool for co-parents. Many communities offer access to family law attorneys, mediation services, and legal aid organizations. These resources can provide personalized advice and support, helping you navigate the complexities of your specific situation. Family law attorneys can offer expert guidance on custody arrangements, visitation schedules, and child support issues. Mediation services provide a neutral third party to facilitate discussions and negotiations, helping both parents reach an agreement in the child's best interest. Legal aid organizations offer free or low-cost legal services to those who qualify, ensuring everyone has the support they need.

Setting up a custody schedule with Custody X Change is a straightforward process. Start by creating an account on the platform and entering the relevant information about both parents and the child. Next, use the parenting plan templates to outline the custody arrangement, including details about visitation schedules, holidays, and vacations. Customize the plan to fit your specific needs, and use the expense-sharing feature to log and track any costs associated with raising the child. Once the plan is complete, you can print or export the documents for use in negotiations or court proceedings. This comprehensive approach ensures that all aspects of the custody arrangement are covered, providing a clear and organized plan that both parents can follow.

Using LegalZoom to draft legal documents is equally simple. Begin by selecting the type of document you need, such as a custody agreement or visitation schedule. LegalZoom provides templates that you can customize with your specific information. Complete the document by following the step-by-step instructions, including all necessary details. LegalZoom offers access to attorneys who can review your documents and provide advice if you need additional guidance. Once the document is complete, you can print and file the document with the appropriate legal authorities once it is full. This process ensures that your legal documents are accurate and compliant with state laws, reducing the risk of disputes or complications.

Finding and consulting with local family law attorneys can provide personalized support tailored to your unique situation. Start by researching attorneys in your area who specialize in family law and custody issues. Many attorneys offer free initial consultations, allowing you to discuss your case and determine if they fit your needs well. Prepare for the consultation by gathering any relevant documentation, such as previous custody agreements, communication records, and financial statements. During the consultation, be open and honest about your situation, and ask any questions you may have. The attorney can guide you on the best course of action, confidently helping you navigate the legal process.

Real-life examples highlight the effectiveness of these legal tools. One parent used Custody X Change to create a comprehensive custody plan. By utilizing the platform's templates and shared calendars, they developed a detailed and organized custody agreement covering all aspects of the child's schedule. The parent presented this plan in court, which helped secure a favorable custody arrangement that prioritized the child's needs.

Another parent resolved legal issues with LegalZoom's help. They drafted a custody agreement and visitation schedule on the platform, ensuring they met all legal requirements. With the assistance of LegalZoom's attorneys, they were able to finalize the documents and file them with the court. This streamlined process reduced stress and provided the parents with the legal support they needed to navigate the complexities of co-parenting.

Local family law resources have also proven invaluable for many parents. One parent sought the assistance of a family law attorney who provided expert guidance on their custody case. The attorney helped them understand their rights and options, offering strategic advice that led to a successful outcome. Mediation services facilitated productive discussions between the parents, resulting in a mutually agreed-upon custody arrangement that benefited the child.

Leveraging these legal tools and resources can significantly enhance your ability to navigate co-parenting. By utilizing Custody X Change, LegalZoom, and local family law resources, you can create and manage custody agreements, access legal forms and documents, and find the legal advice and representation you need. These tools provide the support and guidance necessary to ensure that your co-parenting arrangement is fair, organized, and in your child's best interest.

Utilizing technology and legal tools can transform your co-parenting experience. These resources empower you to handle legal challenges effectively, creating a stable environment for your child. As we move forward, let's explore how to foster resilience and emotional strength in the face of adversity.

CONCLUSION

As we reach the end of this journey together, it's essential to reflect on the challenges, growth, and empowerment that have shaped your path to effective co-parenting with a narcissistic ex. This book was designed to be your guide, offering practical strategies, emotional support, and hope in navigating the complexities of this difficult relationship.

RECAP OF THE JOURNEY

From understanding the traits of narcissism to setting and maintaining boundaries, communicating effectively, and protecting your child's well-being, you've explored a comprehensive toolkit to manage the unique difficulties that come with co-parenting with a narcissist. Each chapter equips you with the knowledge, tools, and confidence to survive and thrive in this journey.

SUMMARIZING THE 9 PRACTICAL STRATEGIES

1. Understanding Narcissism: Recognizing narcissistic traits and their impact on both you and your child is the first step to taking control of the situation.
2. Setting Boundaries: Boundaries are essential to protect your emotional health and maintain a stable environment for your child.
3. Effective Communication: Implementing clear, concise, and non-emotional communication strategies is key to minimizing conflict.
4. Legal Advice and Custody Tips: Being informed about your rights and how to document interactions will empower you in the legal system.
5. Protecting Your Child's Well-Being: Your child's safety and emotional health must be your priority; this chapter provided insights into ensuring both.
6. Self-Care and Emotional Support: You can't pour from an empty cup; taking care of yourself is essential to being an effective co-parent.
7. Personal Empowerment and Growth: Rebuilding your confidence and resilience is crucial to overcoming the psychological impacts of narcissistic abuse.
8. Positive Parenting Techniques: Despite the challenges, positive parenting will foster a strong, loving bond with your child.
9. Support Systems and Resources: You are not alone—tools, communities, and resources are available to support you every step of the way.

KEY TAKEAWAYS

- **Empowerment through Knowledge:** Understanding narcissism and its impact allows you to reclaim your power.
- **Practical Strategies:** Implementing the techniques provided will help you set boundaries, communicate effectively, and protect your child.
- **Emotional Resilience:** Cultivating self-care, building a support network, and focusing on personal growth are vital for your emotional well-being.

REFLECTION

As you close this book, take a moment to reflect on your own journey. Adapt the strategies and insights discussed to fit your unique situation. What resonated most with you? What actions can you take today to strengthen your co-parenting approach and ensure a healthier environment for yourself and your child?

INSPIRE HOPE AND EMPOWERMENT

Remember, you possess the strength and resilience to overcome the challenges of co-parenting with a narcissistic ex. While the road ahead may not be easy, you are not walking it alone. With each step, you are becoming more empowered, more knowledgeable, and more prepared to face whatever comes your way.

CALL TO ACTION

As you move forward, I encourage you to apply the strategies you've learned, seek out the support you need, and continue your journey of growth. Share your experiences with others, join support groups, and never hesitate to seek professional help when necessary. Your journey doesn't end here—it's only the beginning of a more empowered and positive future for you and your child.

ENDING ON AN UPLIFTING NOTE

In the face of adversity, you have shown incredible courage and determination. Despite the obstacles, you are not alone; help is always within reach. Continue to believe in your strength, keep advocating for your well-being and that of your child, and know that brighter days are ahead. We can create a future together where co-parenting becomes a challenge to endure and an opportunity for growth, empowerment, and love. Thank you for allowing me to be part of your journey. I wish you and your child a hope, peace, and happiness-filled future.

REFERENCES

- 10 Best Mental Health and Therapy Apps of 2024 https://www.verywellmind.com/best-mental-health-apps-4692902
- 10 Ways to Practice Self-Care as a Parent https://health.clevelandclinic.org/realistic-ways-to-practice-self-care-as-a-parent
- 14 Confidence Building Activities and Exercises for Adults https://symondsresearch.com/confidence-building-activities/
- 28 Fun Emotional Intelligence Activities for Kids https://veryspecialtales.com/emotional-intelligence-activities-for-kids/
- 59 phrases to help you set boundaries https://www.prdaily.com/59-phrases-to-help-you-set-boundaries/
- 8 Books About Parallel Parenting You Need to Read https://motherhoodandmayhem.online/parallel-parenting-books/
- 8 Ways Gaslighters Manipulate and Control Relationships https://www.psychologytoday.com/us/blog/communication-success/201908/8-ways-gaslighters-manipulate-and-control-relationships
- A Guide to Building a Case Against a Narcissistic Ex https://www.joleenalouislaw.com/blog/a-guide-to-building-a-case-against-a-narcissistic-ex
- Building a Support Network for Coparenting Success https://www.coparentingmastery.com/post/building-a-support-network-for-coparenting-success
- Child Custody: Summaries of State Laws https://www.findlaw.com/family/child-custody/child-custody-summaries-of-state-laws.html
- Community Resources https://firstchanceforchildren.org/resources/community-resources/
- Co-Parenting With a Narcissist: 13 Tips https://www.choosingtherapy.com/co-parenting-with-narcissist/

- Creating a Stable Environment for Children After Divorce https://www.louisvillefamilylaw.com/blog/2020/october/creating-a-stable-environment-for-children-after/
- Custody X Change Software Reviews, Demo & Pricing - 2024 https://www.softwareadvice.com/legal/custody-x-change-profile/
- Effective Co-Parenting: The BIFF Method - Barnhill family law https://barnhillfamilylaw.com/blog/f/effective-co-parenting-the-biff-method?blogcategory=Child+Custody
- Effects of Narcissistic Abuse https://www.verywellmind.com/effects-of-narcissistic-abuse-5208164
- Helping Children Cope With a Narcissistic Parent https://www.psychologytoday.com/us/blog/living-on-automatic/202301/helping-children-cope-with-a-narcissistic-parent
- High-Conflict Divorce & Custody https://www.modernfamilylawfirm.com/family-law/special-circumstances/high-conflict-divorce-and-custody/
- How Google Consumer Apps Can Help a Co-Parenting Plan https://www.theharrisfirmllc.com/2021/07/27/how-googles-consumer-apps-can-help-with-a-co-parenting-plan/
- How Narcissists Retaliate via Procedural and Legal Abuse https://www.psychologytoday.com/us/blog/beyond-cultural-competence/202304/how-narcissists-retaliate-via-procedural-and-legal-abuse
- How To Set Boundaries When Co Parenting With A Narcissist https://drkarenfinn.com/divorce-blog/coparenting/418-how-to-set-boundaries-when-co-parenting-with-a-narcissist/
- How using the grey rock method for co-parenting saved me https://beanstalkmums.com.au/parenting/shared-parenting/grey-rock-method-for-coparenting/
- How to communicate with a narcissist ex about your children https://www.quora.com/How-do-you-communicate-with-a-narcissist-ex-about-your-children
- How to discipline your child the smart and healthy way https://www.unicef.org/parenting/child-care/how-discipline-your-child-smart-and-healthy-way

- How to Find a Narcissistic Abuse Support Group https://www.verywellmind.com/how-to-find-a-narcissistic-abuse-support-group-5271477
- How to Manage Stress with Mindfulness and Meditation https://www.mindful.org/how-to-manage-stress-with-mindfulness-and-meditation/
- How to recognize signs of distress in children https://www.unicef.org/parenting/child-care/how-to-recognize-signs-of-distress
- Narcissistic personality disorder - Symptoms and causes https://www.mayoclinic.org/diseases-conditions/narcissistic-personality-disorder/symptoms-causes/syc-20366662
- Open Communication: Helping Children Through Divorce https://auritmediation.com/open-communication-helping-children-through-divorce/
- Parallel Parenting: Navigating and Understanding Its https://www.verywellmind.com/parallel-parenting-understanding-impact-on-kids-7749955
- Protecting Your Mental Health: Tips for Co-Parents https://talkingparents.com/blog/protecting-your-mental-health
- Reducing Parental Conflict: the impact on children https://www.gov.uk/guidance/reducing-parental-conflict-the-impact-on-children
- Resilience: Build skills to endure hardship https://www.mayoclinic.org/tests-procedures/resilience-training/in-depth/resilience/art-20046311
- Setting Boundaries with a Narcissistic Ex https://www.judgeanthony.com/blog/setting-boundaries-with-a-narcissistic-ex-in-high-conflict-divorce-and-custody-cases
- Setting SMART Goals for Personal Growth: A Step https://thefluentlife.com/content/smart-goals-for-personal-growth/
- Strategies for Successful Co-Parenting With a High-Conflict Ex https://www.bronzinolaw.com/top-10-strategies-for-successful-post-divorce-co-parenting-with-a-high-conflict-ex/

- The Best Co-Parenting Apps of 2024 https://www.thebump.com/a/co-parenting-apps
- Types of Child Custody - Family Law https://www.impactlaw.com/family-law/custody/types
- Why Documentation Is Crucial in Co-Parenting—And How https://www.ourfamilywizard.com/blog/why-documentation-crucial-co-parenting-and-how-do-it

YOUR SUPPORT MEANS THE WORLD TO ME!

Hi there,

I want to personally thank you from the bottom of my heart for choosing *Effective Co-Parenting with a Narcissistic Ex*. Navigating the complexities of co-parenting is not easy, especially when dealing with a challenging ex-partner. The fact that you've taken the time to invest in your growth and your child's well-being is truly inspiring.

When you're finished with the book, I'd love to hear your thoughts! Your honest positive feedback means a lot to me, and it could make a world of difference for other parents who might be facing similar struggles. Reviews play a key role in helping others discover tools that can help them on their journey.

If this book has helped you in any way, or if you have insights you'd like to share, a brief positive review would be so appreciated. It doesn't take long, but it could have a lasting impact on someone else's path.

Thank you again for trusting me to be a part of your co-parenting journey. I'm so grateful for your support and for having you as a reader.

With gratitude,
Stephanie Barnes

www.ingramcontent.com/pod-product-compliance
Lightning Source LLC
LaVergne TN
LVHW092048060526
838201LV00047B/1296